D1560080

# SOLVING THE INNOVATION MYSTERY
## A WORKPLACE WHODUNIT

*STEVE GLADIS*

PRESS

ATD Press is an internationally renowned source of insightful and practical information on talent development, workplace learning, and professional development.

Cover imagery © Shutterstock

**ATD Press**
1640 King Street
Alexandria, VA 22314 USA

Ordering information: Books published by ATD Press can be purchased by visiting ATD's website at www.td.org/books or by calling 800.628.2783 or 703.683.8100.

Library of Congress Control Number: 2016950734

ISBN-10: 1-60728-007-8
ISBN-13: 978-1-60728-007-1
e-ISBN: 978-1-60728-116-0

**ATD Press Editorial Staff**
Director: Kristine Luecker
Manager: Christian Green
Community of Practice Manager, Senior Leaders & Executives: Ann Parker
Developmental Editor: Kathryn Stafford
Senior Associate Editor: Melissa Jones
Cover Design: Tim Green, Faceout Studio
Text Design: John Body
Printed by Data Reproductions Corporation, Auburn Hills, MI

# DISCLAIMER

**The Story**: A work of practice-based fiction, the story describes how creativity and innovation work. As such, all names, characters, places, and incidents are products of the author's imagination or are used fictionally. Any resemblance to actual persons (living or dead), businesses, organizations, events, or locales is entirely coincidental.

**The Research**: This section summarizes some of my research about creativity and innovation, which is offered to inform, motivate, and inspire leaders. It is presented with the understanding that neither the author nor the publisher is engaged in rendering any type of psychological, legal, or any other kind of professional advice.

*For former CEO and chairman of Bonne Bell Cosmetics Jess Bell—an innovator, friend, and mentor. Every time I see 10:06 on the clock, which has happened too many times to count, I think of Jess Bell. The Bell family will know why. Miss you, Jess.*

*Special thanks to my daughter Kimberly Gladis, who helped me to discover the Innovation Equation—the heart of this book. Without her strategic help, I'd still be wandering in the research wilderness.*

# CONTENTS

# ACKNOWLEDGMENTS

I want to thank Donna Gladis, my wife, confidante, and most trusted friend.

Thanks to Kathryn Stafford, my editor at ATD, for her patience, kindness, and skill.

Thanks to those who reviewed an early draft of the book and gave invaluable feedback: Karl Boehm, Mark Colombo, Simon Gillett, Claire Heffernan, Martha Johnson, Piotr Juszkiewicz, Scott Sheafe, Gary Sheehan, Pat Solley, and Randy Yu.

Thanks also to:

- The early morning team at Peet's Coffee & Tea at Kings Park Shopping Center, where I wrote this book in the back every day from 7 to 9 a.m.
- Ann Parker at ATD for moving this project along from start to finish.
- The ATD marketing team, Julia Liapidova, Alex Quinn, and Rachel Soberman, for getting the word out.

# FOREWORD

What do wooden matches, tin cans, and natural fiber rope have in common? The products were made by three American companies, each of which had been in business at least 40 years: the Pennsylvania Match Company, the Continental Can Company, and the Plymouth Cordage Company, respectively.

Each company was a leader in its field. Pennsylvania Match was a highly successful maker of wooden matches. Continental Can made millions of tin cans for food and drinks. Plymouth Cordage was the largest maker of natural fiber rope in the world, supplying all the rope for the U.S. Navy at one time.

These companies have something else in common besides their past success. All three are gone.

And they went out of business for the same reason: They did not adapt and innovate when they needed to. The Pennsylvania Match Company did not add to its product line of wooden stick matches when book matches made of paper were invented. Continental Can, which had been in business for more than 90 years, continued to make tin cans when most of its customers were switching to aluminum cans. And Plymouth Cordage, which had operated for more than 100 years, continued to make natural fiber rope long after it was clear that sailors, firefighters, and mountain climbers preferred rope made from nylon and plastic.

There were of course other reasons why these companies went out of business. But it is clear that their failure to pivot in the face of new developments or to create new products played a big part in their demise. No organization is immune to the need to embrace innovation to survive and grow when market conditions change, or when some new product makes a way of doing business obsolete.

When more than 1,000 CEOs were asked by Pricewaterhouse Coopers (PwC) which global trends would transform their businesses the most over the next five years, three things topped the list: technological advances, demographic shifts, and shifts in global economic power.

Innovation is critical to business success today and companies are slow to embrace it.

Why?

It may have something to do with people and culture. A study that the Association for Talent Development did in partnership with The Ken Blanchard Companies found that innovative companies are more comfortable taking risks and are willing to experiment and celebrate failure. That's not something commonly taught in business school.

The study also found that innovative organizations have innovative environments and are always looking for ways to set themselves apart from the competition. *Competitive advantage* is a term many leaders embrace, but combining it with innovation often leads many to stop in their tracks. For too many leaders, competitive advantage is focused on cutting prices, not creating products that might fail.

Leaders need help understanding what really lies at the heart of creating innovative environments where creative ideas are born and processes exist that can take the ideas and make them innovations. How can we help leaders make this important shift in thinking?

Steve and his daughter Kim Gladis have created a model that helps all of us make this change in thinking. By breaking down innovation into components related to people, environment, and process, they've designed a formula that will help leaders identify areas in their organizations and in their own leadership capabilities that can be improved and honed. The "Innovation Equation" is simple in its components, but the potential it creates when applied is staggering.

In addition, anyone familiar with Steve's impressive body of work knows that he likes to tell a story—and this book is no different. Woven throughout the chapters is a narrative that illustrates the Innovation Equation. It's an unconventional tale, and it drives home Steve's point that innovation is a replicable process available to all of us.

Change is constant. Innovation is imperative. Leaders must know how to manage both, and this book, *Solving the Innovation Mystery*, is a critical read in gaining the capability to systematically deliver the ever-elusive innovation required for organizations to prosper.

—Tony Bingham, President and CEO
Association for Talent Development
Alexandria, Virginia
September 2016

# INTRODUCTION

What happens when you combine an FBI agent, an academic, and a frustrated screenwriter? Sounds like the setup for a joke, right? Actually, it's my story. And it's how I came to write this book.

In my first career, I was an FBI agent, investigating all sorts of stuff, including a stint in counterterrorism; though I can assure you that the work is far less glamorous than what you see on TV programs such as *Criminal Minds* or *The Blacklist*. However, it was a marvelous profession with incredible people dedicated to public safety and law enforcement.

During my tenure as an agent, I also taught at the FBI Academy in Quantico, Virginia, yet another (*Quantico*) FBI-related TV series. While teaching at the FBI Academy, I attended George Mason University and received my doctorate and went on to teach at the University of Virginia and George Mason University. In fact, I still teach at George Mason, and through my own leadership development company I conduct leadership workshops for companies, government agencies, and nonprofits—largely in the Washington, D.C., area. Indeed, leadership has become a true passion of mine.

While teaching at George Mason, my youngest daughter, Jess, convinced me to attend a screenwriting program in Santa Fe, New Mexico. We're both movie lovers, so she thought it could open up some new horizons, which it did. Following the program, I wrote a number of screenplays. But alas, I lived in Northern Virginia, not in Los Angeles, and frankly I'm certainly no Aaron Sorkin (famed screenwriter of *The West Wing* and *Newsroom*.)

All this is to say that a perfect storm converged—my FBI experience, my love of screenwriting, and my passion for leadership—as I began to consider the emergence of innovation as a critical leadership topic. Indeed, you would be hard pressed to open any prominent business journal these days without some essay, article, or complete study about how innovation and competition are reshaping the business and economic landscape. We're all zipping around in a kind of innovation hyper-speed economy in which obsolesce can happen in months, not years.

At the same time, I found that while there was huge interest in innovation, many of my business clients didn't understand how to approach it in a reliable and repeatable way. So I went back to my former FBI mindset, put on my academic hat, and set out to investigate the answer to the question: How can innovation work in a company in a reliable and sustainable way?

I studied what some of the best researchers in the field had to say about innovation so I could relay the innovation story to my clients in a clear, concise, and engaging way. As a child, I was dyslexic, which made me work hard to figure things out. As a result, I've developed a certain ability to clarify complexity and make it accessible to people.

After more than a year of sifting through mounds of data, I was lost, which oftentimes happens when conducting investigations, writing novels, or discovering solutions to a problem. This phenomenon is beautifully explained by Uri Alon in his marvelous TED Talk. You may think that Edison, Disney, da Vinci, and Picasso never lost their way. Think again. A big part of creation and innovation is getting lost and then finding a new path—one that's often more fruitful than the first. If you're really lucky, someone comes along, takes you by the hand, and guides you out of the woods—often to a better path. That guide was my oldest daughter, Kimberly. She's a strategy guru as well as one of most analytical people I know. So, in the midst of being lost, I reached out and asked her if we could get together for a whiteboard session at her office.

I'll not soon forget that three-hour session. Under her direction, we reviewed the evidence I had collected, sorted it, stepped back, and analyzed it. After much thought and discussion, she announced that she saw a theme emerge in the data: "The Innovation Equation!" It was a classic eureka moment that came from putting in a lot of work, which is how all innovation emerges.

Once I sorted and articulated the data, the task of laying out the equation was considerably straightforward. As you'll learn in the coming pages, the innovation equation is Innovation = Talent + Environment + Process. Each of these elements is broken down in detail and explained within the chapters of this book. Although I figured out the organization and presentation of the data, I still needed a story to tell—one that would be realistic, instructive, and entertaining. Remember that screenwriting itch I need to scratch?

It would have been great to have a single story about an average company that did innovation by the book. Unfortunately, such a company does not exist, any more than does the "average reader" of this book. Those reading this book likely come from both large and small companies, nonprofits, and even government agencies. And people come to innovation from many angles; it's rarely an easy process. In fact, that was why I wrote this book. To help illuminate the innovation process, I created a story with some interest, drama, and inspiration. Fables have long been used to help people learn and understand. In modern times, business and leadership fables have been made famous by writers such as Ken Blanchard and Patrick Lencioni. In fact, I have written a number of books in this style, so I'm no stranger to the technique.

However, this time, I wanted to make it even more interesting and challenging. Drawing on my law enforcement background, I thought it would be fun to write a business whodunit story that featured a small but growing company that needed to use innovation to be competitive. Indeed, most companies are small. Even the largest were small at one time, and when they develop a new, innovative product or process, it by nature always starts out small.

In *Solving the Innovative Mystery*, you will be introduced to famed former-detective-turned-private investigator Roland Epps, as he and his former detective partner, Bill Jamison, start and build a business from scratch, morphing and innovating along the way. You'll watch them solve some pretty interesting cases, and you'll see their inevitable frustrations, too. You'll also meet Dana Glass, their amazing coach, who helps them develop their innovation skills, and bring in and develop the right Talent, Environment, and Process (the Innovation Equation) to succeed on the job.

Here's a brief synopsis of the chapters, but also don't miss the executive summary that follows.

*Chapter 1: It's More Than Eureka: The Basics of Innovation* explores the myths of innovation and significant reasons why now is a compelling time to open up your organization to innovation.

*Chapter 2: The Innovation Equation Part 1: Start With Talent* introduces the first element of the Innovation Equation, Talent—people are the bedrock of any organization. This chapter covers three areas: diversity, engagement, and mindset.

*Chapter 3: The Innovation Equation Part 2: Environment* describes the second element of the Innovation Equation, Environment—the organizational soil necessary for talent to be planted, grow, and flourish. The chapter focuses on modern motivational theory and practice—offering a new motivational model of satisfaction, social support, and purpose.

*Chapters 4 and 5: The Innovation Equation Part 3: The Process and The Process Continues* complete the equation by offering the third element of the Innovation Equation, Process, and explaining the theory and practices behind the 5Ps of the Innovation Development Process: problem, present, possible, plan, and pivot.

Let me conclude by saying that I've successfully taught this Innovation Equation to people from federal government agencies to publicly traded corporations to nonprofits. The results are always the same: Attendees all have their own eureka moments as they begin to understand what innovation is all about and how to make the magic happen consistently and reliably.

# EXECUTIVE SUMMARY

Many executives have a need to read books but little time to do so. For them I've included an executive summary of the nonfiction concepts of this book.

> The crux of this book is that to remain competitive in a fast-paced, global, and ever-changing world, the best leaders create an intentional culture of innovation. To create such a culture, leaders need to understand the Innovation Equation:
>
> **Innovation = Talent + Environment + Process**

There isn't a CEO who hasn't thought about the importance of innovation in the face of global competition and advances in technology. In a virtual and fast-moving world, companies must become more adaptive and competitive or go out of business. The question is, how do you grow new innovations systematically and reliably while still producing the products and services that make money to keep the lights on and pay employees? How does a company remain both productive and adaptive?

Ask any group of people to define *creativity* and *innovation* and their lists will likely be nearly identical. In reality, those terms are as different as activity versus results. For purposes of this book, let's differentiate creativity and innovation by using an expert, plain-spoken definition: Creativity is about coming up with the big idea. Innovation is about executing on the idea—converting the idea into a successful business proposition of value (Govindarajan 2010). In the case of public service organizations and nonprofits, it's about creating value of a different sort—a better city, classroom, or congregation.

After studying the research on innovation, I came up with the following Innovation Equation: **Innovation = Talent + Environment + Process (I = T + E + P)**. This book explores each of these elements.

# Talent

The first factor in the Innovation Equation is Talent. All creativity starts with talent—people with creative ideas. Talent is composed of at least three critical, but not necessarily exclusive, elements: diversity, engagement, and mindset.

## Diversity

People with similar backgrounds gathered together in a corporate conference room effectively create an "echo chamber"—they agree with themselves, rather than testing their ideas with the outside world, especially their customers. This approach is a surefire way to miss the mark every time. The antidote for creating an echo chamber is cognitive diversity—having diverse people who think differently work together to tackle a problem or opportunity from varying points of view. One way to approach cognitive diversity might be to randomly select people to work on an innovative project. Another way is to use one of several good personality instruments, such as the Myers-Briggs Type Indicator (MBTI).

## Engagement

Gallup has researched and documented that engaged people produce as much as 30 percent more than their less motivated, less engaged colleagues. Engagement is tied to utilizing one's strengths—talent themes that have been well developed into high-functioning strengths. For example, when analytical engineers work on complex problems that require them to use their problem-solving skills regularly, they are more innovative, more productive, and generally happier. Taking Gallup's StrengthsFinder assessments provides an excellent window into both individual and team strengths.

## Mindset

What's the difference between failing and learning? Your mindset! According to Carol Dweck, renowned Stanford University psychologist, it all boils down to whether you think of talent and intelligence as a fixed ability or one that can be developed through effort and practice. Often it comes down to whether you seek validation or a challenge. Whether you look at people on teams, at work, at school, or in any relationships, the fixed-versus-growth mindset is a very important concept to understand if you want to enhance creativity and innovation.

# Environment

The second factor in the Innovation Equation is Environment. All innovation starts with an idea generated by a person, but nobody generates anything unless they're working in a motivating environment. So if you want to prepare and cultivate innovation in your organization, start with what motivates people to create any new product or service. To explore such cultures, consider these two exceptional motivators: Abraham Maslow and Frederick Herzberg. After relating their theories to modern-day research on the power that social setting has on innovation, a new model emerges: the Motivation Pyramid + the Motivation Matrix.

## The Motivation Pyramid

The Motivation Pyramid has three critical steps: Satisfaction, Social, and Purpose (Figure 1).

**1. Satisfaction:** People have to feel safe and have their needs met. They need to be paid well and have adequate benefits, such as healthcare and time off; have a good place to work; have a leader they respect; have the freedom to experiment, fail, and learn; and feel secure.

**2. Social:** People need to belong—to have co-workers to share their ideas with and teammates who will support them through success and especially through failure. Otherwise, a sense of perspective gets lost in isolation.

**3. Purpose:** People need stimulation and motivation—a sense of purpose—that pushes them through the ups and downs of trial, error, and discovery. Without the stimulation of real purpose, the flame of motivation goes out and produces a mindset to simply "put in time" at work.

Figure 1: The Motivation Pyramid

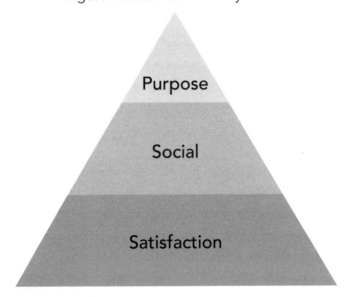

## The Motivation Matrix

When a person comes up with a creative, adaptive idea, the easy part is done. But to scale an idea into an innovation, it takes more people—motivated ones. Specifically, for an innovation to be successful, a creative idea must scale from people to teams to organizations—each of which is necessary to grow innovation into profitability.

This migration from people to teams to organizations is the Motivation Matrix (Table 1). When leaders establish a motivational environment, they're ready for the third step of the Innovation Equation—the 5Ps Innovation Development Process.

Table 1: The Motivation Matrix

| The Motivation Pyramid | People | Teams | Organizations |
|---|---|---|---|
| *Purpose* | Purpose Driven | Mission Focused | Vision Centric |
| *Social* | Socially Connected | Socially Collaborative | Culturally Integrated |
| *Satisfaction* | Needs Met | Team Supported | Organizationally Stable |

# The 5Ps Innovation Development Process

The third factor in the Innovation Equation is Process. Once you have good ideas and a motivating and nurturing environment, then innovation requires a reliable and repeatable process. Combining the research from three powerful and proven areas—coaching, action learning, and entre-preneurship—a hybrid innovation model, the 5Ps Innovation Develop-ment Process, emerges that is both reliable and repeatable. It is a process that helps teams and organizations produce innovations.

In a nutshell, the 5Ps Innovation Development Process consists of asking questions that elicit thinking, reflection, and discussion. Next, innovative leaders and coaches need a process or framework to help shep-herd their teams through a cycle that can produce change. Employing the leader-as-coach approach, the process involves the five steps of the 5Ps: problem, present, possible, plan, and pivot (Figure 2).

Figure 2: The 5Ps Innovation Development Process

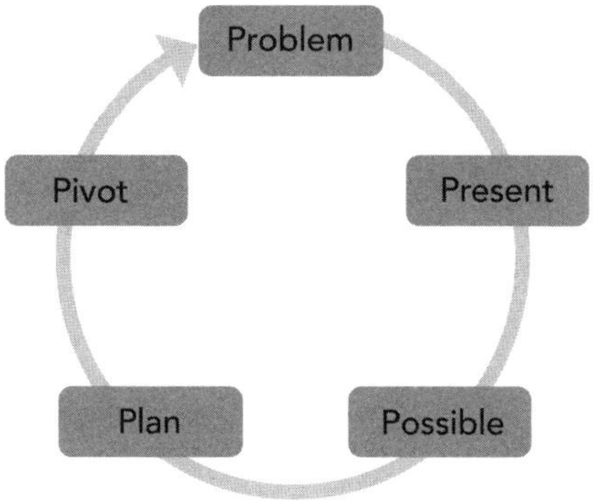

1. **Problem:** The leader or coach ensures that the first round of questions in this process works toward framing a precise description of the problem, issue, or opportunity that has presented itself.
2. **Present:** Teams need to conduct an inventory of the present state of the problem before moving to the next step. What's the present state? Who's involved? What's the cost of doing nothing?
3. **Possible:** Staying open to all that's possible is difficult for some people, but the leader or coach pushes the team to take off their blinders. What does the ideal possible future look like? Who will be involved?
4. **Plan:** The leader or coach challenges the team to take action, if only to take a small first step. Taking big steps often intimidates people. So the leader or coach asks people to take one manageable step at a time.
5. **Pivot:** This is what often happens after the first meeting. The issue gets modified by experience, creating a new iteration of the problem or opportunity to redefine it for a future meeting.

If you want to innovate—for example, start a new business or add a new product or service to an existing business—remember the Innovation Equation:

$$\text{Innovation} = \text{Talent} + \text{Environment} + \text{Process}$$

# Reference

Govindarajan, V. 2010. "Innovation Is Not Creativity." *Harvard Business Review*, August 3. https://hbr.org/2010/08/innovation-is-not-creativity.html.

# 1

# IT'S MORE THAN EUREKA: THE BASICS OF INNOVATION

We often think of innovation as a single genius having a eureka moment that happens overnight. In essence, we think it's like a hero conquering a difficult foe, overcoming all odds to win—a hero's journey. There's one problem: It just doesn't happen that way. Innovation is collaborative: It takes a village; it takes time; it involves failure and retrying over and over.

Scott Berkun, speaker, author, and former Microsoft executive, raises some keen observations on the subject of innovation in his book *The Myths of Innovation*. According to Berkun, though you may admire the brain power of Newton, Edison, Jobs, or Gates, it's clear that discovery comes from hard work, risk, and sacrifice, not some divine epiphany. Furthermore, innovation does not have a straight-line trajectory, nor does it happen overnight. In fact, many inventors aren't considered geniuses until after they die. Rather, such monumental inventions—the radio, television, laser, and the computer, for example—were accumulations of ideas and efforts over time.

Small insights lead to big breakthroughs. Walter Isaacson, author of *The Innovators: How a Group of Hackers, Geniuses, and Geeks Created the Digital Revolution*, admits that writers have to resist the temptation of telling the hero tale in favor of the less sexy, slower moving truth— that it "takes a village" to innovate. Moreover, innovators stand on the shoulders not only of their teams but also of their historical predecessors.

The creative "epiphany" is really much more like putting the final piece of the puzzle together than it is magic. When you put the last piece in place, it may feel like magic, but it's the result of trial and error. Because fantasy, not reality, sells, writers often call up eureka-type stories to explain the arduous task of evolving innovations. It's like watching an exciting TV drama about smart, dedicated, and attractive lawyers fighting in court and then comparing it to the grueling real-life version of practicing law.

That's why we read biographies of people like Steve Jobs. We hope to find the magic or secret to the next big thing. But that's not how it works. Like Jobs, innovators are human, warts and all. Romanticizing them can take you down a rabbit hole. According to Berkun, we think of Edison as the inventor of electricity, Apple the inventor of the digital music player, and Google the inventor of the search engine. But they were not; rather, they came after a long chain of "connections."

Innovation comes from experimentation, failure, learning, more experimentation, more failure, and finally, maybe one day, breakthrough. And it takes many people and much trial and error—not a singular hero or eureka moment in the middle of the night—to make innovation happen.

## The Creative Process

In his book *Little Bets: How Breakthrough Ideas Emerge From Small Discoveries*, Peter Sims writes, "The best entrepreneurs don't begin with brilliant ideas—they discover them." Sims tells the stories of creative geniuses such as John Legend, Thomas Edison, and Jeff Bezos as examples of people who placed a number of small bets (investments of time, talent, and money) to test their ideas early on. They all used what can be called an emergent design. Indeed, discovery is neither a linear process, nor is knowledge static—even though some textbooks might have us believe those linear, logical notions.

Sims talks about what comedian Chris Rock and Amazon's Bezos, among others, have in common. They make little bets along the way—they experiment. Rock, for example, literally takes a notepad into little off-the-beaten-path comedy clubs and tries out his jokes with small, die-hard comedy audiences. And only when he perfects his jokes does he use them on TV or in front of large groups. Bezos was convinced that people would buy books online, so he started Amazon on a bet; though he failed several times along the way. For example, his failed partnership with Sotheby's, when he went head to head with eBay, stands out as one of his biggest failed bets. Sims's theory of experimental innovation actually comes from a number of seemingly unrelated places: the military, creative artists, entrepreneurs, software developers, and more. Sims observes and urges "design thinking" based on building up answers from experimenting and observations rather than starting with the correct answer.

## Three Data Points

Consider the following three data points about the importance of innovation: First, innovation is the lifeblood of our global economy. In fact, an IBM global study of 1,500 CEOs from 60 countries and 33 industries asked the CEOs to identify the number one factor for success for the future of business. Overwhelmingly, they said "creativity." To remain competitive in a global economy, CEOs recognize that their future leaders will have to be able to not only think creatively but also innovate on an idea and produce a new, needed product or service.

Second, in one of his bestselling books, *A Whole New Mind: Why Right-Brainers Will Rule the Future*, Dan Pink argues that as we move from an information age to a conceptual age, we will need to think differently to thrive and in some cases even survive. And key among "six senses," or ways of thinking, he notes that people—especially leaders—of the future will have to engage in design thinking, which is creative thinking that makes things not only functional but also engaging by their very nature. Think about how beautiful and engaging Apple's products are—a great example of form and function at its best. Pink's key argument: We're already outsourcing left-brain functions. These days, you can hardly have a conversation with major CEOs who do not outsource some or much of their programming or tech support to India, the Philippines, or somewhere other than the United States, anywhere where labor costs are minimal. Basically, Pink argues that it's becoming far easier to commoditize such left-brain processes. However, he identifies design thinking (creativity) as a more artfully conceptual, right-brained task, which becomes a competitive advantage; one that's of higher value and difficult to commoditize.

Third, these days we're no longer just competing in a local, state, or national economic race; we're competing in a much larger global arena. And the game gets much more competitive as you move up the ladder of keen competition—much like being able to play football in high school, then maybe, just maybe being able to play in college, but having a very, very slim chance of playing in the pros. As the competitive stakes get higher and higher, the secret weapon is creativity and innovation.

## Creativity Versus Innovation

We know that innovation is not creativity, but these terms are often confused. As author and professor Vijay Govindarajan writes, "Creativity is about coming up with the big idea. Innovation is about executing the idea—converting the idea into a successful business." To be sure, creativity and innovation are closely joined, yet distinct. Indeed, creativity without execution is simply a good idea with no real legs. And most people, teams, and companies are far better at generating ideas than they are at commercializing them.

However, execution and commercialization remain at the heart of innovation. Leaders who want to stay competitive must create a culture that supports and influences employees, teams, and entire organizations to move from creativity to innovation. Culture has been best described as "the way we do things around here" driven by a host of behaviors, habits, and customs unique to a particular group. Thus, every family, team, company, and organization has its own particular way of operating. Culture protects organizations and the people in them by preserving the status quo. In essence, culture acts like the immune system—protecting the company from any new "virus" that may enter and potentially harm the organization. The operating hypothesis of culture is that what got you here is likely to continue to work. It's a good hypothesis for the short term but not a particularly good long-term strategy—especially in a volatile, uncertain environment, like the world we now live in where business changes as fast as the weather. Think about companies that once thrived but did not innovate, such as Kodak and Borders, to name just two on a very long list. In fact, over the past 20 years the Dow Jones index, which tracks how 30 major publicly owned companies based in the United States have traded, has dropped 19 companies from its prestigious list for lack of performance.

## Why Is Innovation Important to Leaders?

Leaders have power, and power is a strong influencer. Robert Cialdini has spent a lifetime thinking about influence and persuasion. After studying both social science research and practice in fields such as sales and marketing, Cialdini settled on six major influencers in life:

1. reciprocity (we feel indebted if someone does something for us)
2. commitment and consistency (we like to stay the course if we've agreed to something)
3. consensus (what do those around us think?)
4. liking (we like to agree with those we know or who are like us)
5. authority (we respect the opinions of experts)
6. scarcity (if we lack something, we value it more).

The power of authority should be understood by leaders to effectively foster a climate and culture that stimulates creativity, which leads to innovation in the workplace. In many experiments, Cialdini notes that few people will question authority. In fact, the most notorious example of overriding power comes from World War II German concentration camps where many Nazi soldiers claimed what is now called the Nuremberg defense—"Befehl ist Befehl," or orders are orders—and that a soldier should not be punished for following orders from a superior officer. Of course, that defense failed.

In the wake of the Nuremberg trials, experiments have proven that indeed people—at their own peril—often blindly follow orders from an authority. That said, leaders must understand the power they have. Their words are heard as shouts and their suggestions as orders. Thus, when a new CEO says, "my office is a bit dark," she should not be so surprised if she finds people repainting her office the next day.

Indeed, a leader can quite literally change the emotional "weather" in an organization with a single word or a gesture. As social beings and herd animals, we constantly read the demeanor of leaders for signals about what they like and don't, and adjust quickly to please them. If a leader gives off negative signs, we narrow focus (based on the threat—his or her disaffection) and adjust to either change course or get out of the area to a safer place.

According to David Rock, author of *Your Brain at Work: Strategies for Overcoming Distraction, Regaining Focus, and Working Smarter All Day Long*, there are five social emotions that, to the brain, feel like either basic survival threats or rewards, depending on if they're presented positively or negatively (a reward or a threat). Here are the five social emotions and what they might look like as threats from a leader:

1. **Status:** When anyone, especially a leader, threatens the status of another by being disrespectful, boasting, or acting superior, other people are also threatened and they become defensive.
2. **Certainty:** When a leader comes into a new organization, his or her mere arrival threatens the certainty of others and defenses go up until people determine that the new leader is "safe."
3. **Autonomy:** When a leader tells people what to do and makes demands instead of asking questions, autonomy gets threatened and people resist; micromanagement is an absolute toxin.
4. **Relatedness:** When a leader appears to exclude people or distrust them, relatedness gets threatened and prisoner thinking (survival of self only) takes over.
5. **Fairness:** When people feel or see others around them unfairly treated, they will want to right the wrong with a vengeance. People are finely tuned to fairness and consistency.

However, when the leader reacts positively, followers relax, open up, and become more adaptive and creative. The feeling of safety created by the leader changes everything, especially people's willingness to experiment, take chances, and create. In short, as management expert and professor Kim Cameron says, we're heliotropic. From one-celled creatures to humans, we're attracted to light, warmth, and positivity, and repelled by dark, cold, and negativity. Leaders are at the epicenter of creating an innovative, positive culture that ultimately leads to adaptation and competitiveness in a changing, and often uncertain, world.

So what does this mean to foster a culture of innovation? With positive leaders, creativity increases—people feel safe and open to opportunities. With negative leaders, creativity gets stifled—people feel unsafe and focus on survival. In short, a safe, trusting, positive culture is essential for thriving creativity, where all innovation starts.

Whether people are in a small or large business, they have to feel safe to create. Safe cultures produce innovations—novel products and services that create value. Being free to question the status quo well before it becomes the very anchor that pulls down the company is critical to corporate competitiveness and even survival in today's markets. Companies that ensure this kind of culture disrupt their industries and competitors.

In the story that follows you'll watch a small business—a detective agency—evolve. Its leader is a creative guy, Roland Epps, who for years was "trapped" in a police department that didn't value his creativity, independent thought, or novel approaches to crime fighting. Now free from those restraints, Roland has decided to build the kind of business in which creativity and innovation can happen—in a free, open, and safe environment.

## THE STORY: Innovative Investigations

Small insights lead to big breakthroughs. This is what Roland Epps always told himself. Here he was living the dream. Newly retired from the metropolitan police department, his own boss now, he could take the cases he wanted—the ones that were fun—rewarding his deeply observant nature. Life wasn't predictable, far from it, but former Detective First Class Roland Epps wasn't usually taken by surprise.

He wasn't surprised when the department forced him into this early retirement; he'd seen it happen to more decorated officers. Or when his longtime partner Bill decided to join him in this new venture rather than take on a department newbie; that was just how loyal Bill was. But entering his second 50, as Roland liked to think of his recent birthday, and his relationship with Bill being the longest—either professional or personal—of Roland's life, had caught him by surprise.

Today, as he walked through the glass doors of the Mason Enterprise Center, the temp on the desk, a student at George Mason University, smiled broadly and said, "Hello, Mr. Epps," with a kind of upward lilt that invited his smile and response, "Hey, Gretchen."

At 6'2", with silver, wavy hair, the 50-year-old detective had a movie-star quality, but those in the police department who dared call him "Hollywood"—as much for the roles he'd played to crack cases as for his good looks—whispered it behind his back.

Then they would tell the story about the time Roland feigned falling asleep in an interview with the notorious gang leader Willie B. Cartle. The hot-headed young thug got so angry that he yelled at his interrogator to wake up. When Roland "woke up," he asked, "Who the hell are you?"

Willie B angrily screwed up his face, looking vile enough to bite. "Who the hell am I?" he repeated. After a second's pause, Willie B bellowed, "Tell you who I am, d-e-t-e-c-t-i-v-e," each singsong syllable punching the air of the small interrogation room. Then he paused again, rethinking the situation.

Detective Epps, reclined again, said, "OK, son. Who are you?"

"I ain't your son, for real."

"So, who are you—tough guy?"

"Just ask that teller at the bank."

"Bank teller?" Detective Epps looked puzzled, feigning confusion from being awakened so rudely.

Willie B's eyes would have punched Epps if they had fists.

"The bank?" Epps asked again.

"Yeah, the fool at the bank I stuck up!"

Following Willie B's rather hard-pitched, inadvertent confession, Detective Epps rolled down his shirt sleeves, smoothed out the wrinkles, and buttoned both cuffs. Next, he fastened his shirt collar and straightened his silk striped tie. He pulled on a pair of titanium wire-rimmed glasses that had been in his shirt pocket and hooked them over his ears; neatly in place, they changed his face in a way that made him look far more alert, even studious.

Then as he rose, the detective pulled on his cashmere sport coat, grabbed the tape recorder from his jacket pocket, and turned it off. Towering over the table and Willie B, Detective Epps smiled faintly and said, "Thanks for your assistance, Mr. Cartle. That's all I needed to know. Have a nice day."

"Damn!" Willie B said loud enough for the detectives behind the one-way glass to hear. They were laying odds on how long it would take Roland Epps to get a confession this time. He was a legend in the department and a great source of entertainment.

During his days with the police department, Roland also taught interviewing and interrogation for the criminal justice program at George Mason University. Then when he retired, he secured office space nearby at the Mason Enterprise Center—an incubator for new businesses in the City of Fairfax. Roland loved the place—young and old entrepreneurs bustling around like their hair was on fire—many working on the next big thing in technology or developing some new business model or innovation—all living out their dreams.

Almost two months after he retired, Roland was joined by his old partner on the force, Bill Jamison. Short, squat, and balding, Bill was blunt and quiet to the point of being introverted, while Roland was articulate and gregarious. Bill was practical, down to earth, and traditional—a gumshoe kind of detective—and Roland highly intuitive and creative. Yes, they were opposites, but as partners for many years they had worked well together. So it was no surprise that following his retirement, Bill joined Roland in the new firm: Epps Security—Private Investigators.

# Enter the Executive Coach

Not long after opening the doors of Epps Security, cases were coming in at a steady pace as friends and colleagues referred more clients the detectives' way. In fact, Roland and Bill had already begun talking about adding more staff and expanding. Yet while Roland favored having fun and generating more creative investigative techniques, Bill opted for measured, but steady growth.

"We're gonna have to pull in more people to keep up with the calls or just say no to clients, who will go elsewhere," Bill said.

"I hear you," said Roland. "Just not sure I want to deal with all the issues of growth—all the logistics, management. I'm for keeping it small and creative and fun."

But the two partners had been having this discussion most every week now, and it was creating a bit of a wedge in their relationship. One day, Roland said, "Look, I've called up an old friend to have lunch with us. Her name is Dana Glass—she's an executive coach."

So the two partners arranged to meet Dana at a small and reasonable local Vietnamese restaurant, the Eastwind. Roland noticed a few heads turn as Dana entered and made her way to their table. Confident and understated, she held out her hand and Roland smoothly maneuvered her to the chair near his.

The two had met a few years ago at a Fall for the Book event at the university—they were both detective fiction fans, and now Dana reached into her large burnished leather tote, whose amber color matched the highlights in her hair, and spread four early George V. Higgins novels out on the table.

"Crime novels—to celebrate your new career. I remember how much you like Higgins. You haven't read these have you?"

"I've always meant to read this," Roland said, picking up *Kennedy for the Defense*. "Thanks, Dana, I'm not a smart lawyer like this guy, but I'll enjoy it."

"It's the criminal conversation, Roland, the banter, like I imagine you have with . . ."

"Criminals?" He raised his eyebrows in mock alarm.

"I bet you're good at it." She smiled and pushed the book toward him on the table. "Now, so why are we here?"

After introductions, Bill asked point blank, "So, Dana, how does this executive coaching stuff work?"

Just then a waiter breezed up to the table with menus and glasses of water, made eye contact with Roland and grinning, asked, "Two or three?"

Roland held up three fingers then turned to his lunch mates, "Guys, three orders of crispy spring rolls enough? They're the best."

Dana nodded and smiled at Roland, then took a moment to sip her water and collect her thoughts after the interruption and said, "Rather than tell you, Bill, I'll show you—if that's OK?"

The partners nodded almost in sync.

Dana asked point blank, "OK, so what's the biggest problem or opportunity you guys are facing today?"

The conversation bounced back to the creativity and fun-or-growth debate.

Bill began, "Maybe that last recession made me cautious, but—" before Roland cut in. "Nah, you've been cautious forever, since I've known you at least. Face it, for better or worse, fun or growth defines who we are."

"But it doesn't have to," Dana said. "What makes them exclusive?"

Both Roland and Bill looked at each other and laughed, and Roland said, "Nothing at all, I guess." Bill nodded in agreement.

"So then, is it fair to say that the question might be how can you balance both creativity and growth in your agency and continue to prosper?"

The partners looked sideways at each other and grudgingly nodded.

Next, Dana asked them about the present state of the problem or opportunity they faced and what would be the impact of either resolving or not resolving it.

Bill looked down at the menu on the table and Roland off in the distance. Ultimately, Roland admitted, doing nothing, the company would languish; there would be simple, one-off cases, no growth to any scale, and they'd remain a "lifestyle" kind of company.

"Is that OK with you both? Having a lifestyle company?" Dana asked.

"Not really," Bill said quickly without looking over at his partner. "I've especially wanted the company to grow."

"What's behind your desire to grow the company, Bill?" Dana asked.

"My Dad had always wanted me to go into business. Said I was a natural. But I became attracted to law enforcement somehow. Now I want to try the business thing."

Dana listened, then asked, "How about you, Roland?"

"I'm good either way as long as I get a chance to 'act,'" Roland said, gesturing with air quotes. "I love being creative—gets my juices flowing. So, I'm good to grow the company but not if it gets overprocessed. I need room to breathe."

Then Dana asked, "What might the best possible future for Epps Security look like in three to five years?"

This led to a lot of head scratching and "good question" comments from the two former detectives. Dana kept a list of their collective comments to this question on a paper napkin that looked like this:

- ABOUT 5–10 PEOPLE ON THE PAYROLL DOING INTERESTING WORK. YOUNG FOLKS IN THEIR 20–30s AND SOME OLDER.
- A FEW PAID ASSISTANTS FROM GEORGE MASON UNIVERSITY—GRADUATE OR PROFESSIONAL STUDENTS IN CRIMINAL JUSTICE, IT, LAW, AND BUSINESS.
- THE FIRM'S REPUTATION WOULD GROW AND BE IN DEMAND BY MORE SOPHISTICATED CORPORATIONS.
- FINANCES WOULD BE STABLE AND THE BUSINESS MODEL WOULD MATURE AND BE MORE PREDICTABLE, REPLICABLE.

Next, Dana asked about their plan going forward—what were these two partners willing to do next? When would they do it? Would they let her know when they got things done?

They thought that contacting the School of Business at George Mason might make a lot of sense to find out about prospective student hires.

They agreed to do it in the next two weeks and then email Dana.

Dana agreed, then asked the final question, "So what's one thing of value you got from our discussion today?"

They both looked at each other, and Roland said, "I think this is the first time we've ever seriously discussed the future. We've been just putting one foot in front of the other. Sure, we're making money, but we're slogging along instead of having a real purpose drive the company.

To which Bill added, "Amen!"

"Great," Dana said. "At the beginning of lunch, Bill asked about how coaching worked."

She then explained: "Good coaches ask questions that make people slow down, think, and reflect. People closest to the problem are always the ones most likely to be able to solve it. Coaches work clients through a deliberative thought process that looks like this:

- problem (define the issue/problem)
- present status (what does the problem look like right now)
- possible future state (what will the future look like if it goes well)
- plan (what steps are clients willing to take to get started).

Then Dana paused, smiled, and said, "You've just been coached."

For years, Roland had kept a black leather notebook for cases and all sorts of ideas he had. Before the three left, he made a few notes:

> **Roland's Notes**
>
> ☐ Ask questions if you want to get information and solve problems.
> ☐ Who, what, how, open-ended questions.
> ☐ Who are we?
> ☐ Problem, present state, possible future, plan.
> ☐ How can we innovate?
> ☐ Creativity is more than eureka.

# References

Berkun, S. 2010. *The Myths of Innovation*. Sebastopol, CA: O'Reilly Media.

Cameron, K. 2012. *Positive Leadership: Strategies for Extraordinary Performance*. 2nd ed. San Francisco: Berrett-Koehler.

Cialdini, R.B. 2006. *Influence: The Psychology of Persuasion*. Rev. ed. New York: Harper Business.

Dyer, J., H. Gregersen, and C.M. Christensen. 2011. *The Innovator's DNA: Mastering the Five Skills of Disruptive Innovators*. Boston: Harvard Business Review Press.

Govindarajan, V. 2010. "Innovation Is Not Creativity." *Harvard Business Review*, August 3. https://hbr.org/2010/08/innovation-is-not-creativity.html.

———, and C. Trimble. 2010. *The Other Side of Innovation: Solving the Execution Challenge*. Boston: Harvard Business Review Press.

IBM Institute for Business Value. 2010. "Capitalizing on Complexity: Insights From the Global Chief Executive Officer Study." Somers, NY: IBM Global Business Services. www 01.ibm.com/common/ssi/ cgi- bin/ssialias?subtype=XB&infotype=PM&appname=GBSE_GB_TI_ USEN&htmlfid=GBE03297USEN&attachment=GBE03297USEN.PDF.

Isaacson, W. 2014. *The Innovators: How a Group of Hackers, Geniuses, and Geeks Created the Digital Revolution*. New York: Simon & Schuster.

Pink, D.H. 2005. *A Whole New Mind: Why Right-Brainers Will Rule the Future*. New York: Penguin.

Rock, D. 2009. *Your Brain at Work: Strategies for Overcoming Distraction, Regaining Focus, and Working Smarter All Day Long*. New York: HarperCollins.

Serchuk, D. 2009. "The Dead Dogs of the Dow." *Forbes*, September 30. www. forbes.com/2009/09/30/dead-dogs-dow-intelligent-investing-index.html.

Sims, P. 2011. *Little Bets: How Breakthrough Ideas Emerge From Small Discoveries*. New York: Simon & Schuster.

# 2

# THE INNOVATION EQUATION PART I: START WITH TALENT

To remain competitive in a fast-paced, global, and ever-changing world, the best leaders create an intentional culture of innovation. Creativity is about coming up with the big idea. Innovation is about executing on the idea—converting the idea into a successful business proposition of value. In the case of public service organizations and nonprofits, it's about creating value of a different sort—a better city, classroom, or congregation.

After studying the research on innovation, I developed the Innovation Equation: **Innovation = Talent + Environment + Process (I = T+ E + P)**. This book explores each of those elements. Let's start with Talent.

All creativity, and ultimately innovation, starts with talent—people experimenting. Someone has to have an idea—born out of necessity or fantasy—and then test that idea in an experiment. Imagine the Wright brothers first talking about flight, the scientists at DARPA (Defense Advanced Research Projects Agency) first discussing the Internet, or Jeff Bezos first talking about selling books and all manner of items online. One can only imagine people reacting to these early creative ideas: "Are you nuts?!"

Everything we do in life is an experiment and a potentially creative act of sorts. When you get up in the morning and decide what to eat for breakfast, you may pick the same old thing you eat every day or combine a set of foods and create a new meal. You may put sliced kiwi on cereal, slap some peanut butter on a banana, or spread some Greek yogurt on a bagel. When you look at the weather on your iPhone and see a 60 percent chance of rain, you may decide to put on an older pair of shoes, wear a raincoat, or take an umbrella. It's all an experiment to help you adapt to your life—creatively. And one day the experiment works, another day it doesn't, so you try something different—all in service of a better, more adaptive life.

The same thing happens in a company. Every great invention first starts as an idea in someone's brain—usually as a question—like, "I wonder what happens when you combine chocolate and peanut butter?" No doubt something like this was the question and the experimentation that launched Reese's Peanut Butter Cups—now a billion-dollar product for Hershey's. Or take ergonomic gardening tools, an entire industry that has developed from research into how our different bodies fit with the environment and can be accommodated in the world around us. Or YouTube, which combined simple videos with the web to create an amazing video-sharing site. There are as many such varied questions and experiments as there are circumstances of people meeting life head on. None of us thinks or behaves the same way. If you've been married for more than an hour, worked for more than one manager in your life, or ever been part of any team, you realize the truth of this statement.

Here's how *Webster's* dictionary defines creativity: "The ability to make new things or think of new ideas." Simple enough. But when you start to figure out what affects individual creativity, the game gets tougher. Scanning the research, the following three areas are offered as bedrock for creative talent: diversity, engagement, and mindset.

## Diversity

The surest way to flub up the launch of a new product or service is to invent it in a back room with a bunch of people—all with the same type of personality—the "echo-chamber" effect. When you have an idea and share it with someone very similar to yourself, it's often a lot like yelling in a canyon and hearing your own voice coming back in an echo—saying essentially: "Great idea. I love it." Problem is that voice is your own and by nature is biased. Cognitive diversity stands as the single-best antidote to such a potentially costly error. Chances are pretty good that if you randomly survey every third person on a busy street for an hour for their collective opinion, you'd get better results than having a half-dozen colleagues—all with the same education, background, and vested interests talking to each other in a corporate conference room.

Cognitive diversity focuses on the effects of divergent personalities looking at the same problem or opportunity from different points of view. One of many personality models to explore, and perhaps the best known, is the Myers-Briggs Type Indicator. Building on the work of Carl Jung, Katharine Cook Briggs and her daughter Isabel Briggs Myers—with the help of the Educational Testing Service—developed the Myers-Briggs Type Indicator, probably the world's most popular personality self-assessment indicator. Without a full-blown explanation of the instrument (covered in my earlier book *WriteType*), there are two fundamentally different kinds of thinkers in the cognitive domain.

1. **Intuitors**: These folks are good at synthesis. They're most at home when they collect, connect, and synthesize to create something new. These folks brought you mocha Frappuccinos, iPads, and hardtop convertibles. They're constantly asking: What's new? What if? Why? Why not? They're big-picture, big-idea, high-concept people. They're most comfortable living in the world of the mind and ideas. Only about 25 percent of people think this way. They are naturally creative and will be in high demand in the world of innovation. Best advice when dealing with intuitors: Trust their vision and ideas, but test their data. They need to be grounded in reality by the sensors group.

2. **Sensors**: These folks like to analyze, break down, inspect, and change (adapt) to something new—like an engineer. Sensors love data—the more the better. They're not afraid of data or documentation. In fact, they lust after it! Trust them with numbers and details—but not necessarily with coming up with the next new thing or a new strategy moving toward the future.

They're all about maintaining and modifying, incremental change, but not coming up with the next new thing—a radical, transformational change.

## Entrepreneurs and Creativity

What about those people who create a lot—entrepreneurs? In *The Innovator's DNA: Mastering the Five Skills of Disruptive Innovators*, Jeff Dyer, Hal Gregersen, and Clayton Christensen uncovered the origins of innovative, disruptive business ideas and the people who create those ideas. Ultimately, their goal was to explore the minds of innovative leaders and extract a formula for innovative success—what made them "think different," as Steve Jobs said.

The authors studied 100 revolutionary founders and executives like Jeff Bezos (Amazon), Pierre Omidyar (eBay), Steve Jobs (Apple), and Marc Benioff (Salesforce.com). They focused on four types of innovators: start-up entrepreneurs; corporate entrepreneurs, who lead an innovative venture from within a corporation; product innovators, who invent a new product; and process innovators, who launch a revolutionary process. They also collected self-reported data and 360-degree data on discovery skills from more than 500 innovators and more than 5,000 executives in more than 75 countries. In their study, the authors were careful to select *innovative entrepreneurs* over entrepreneurs, pointing out that earlier entrepreneurship research classified entrepreneurs in general as not significantly different (on personality traits or psychometric measures) from typical business executives. But using the authors' definition, only 10 to 15 percent of entrepreneurs are innovators.

Following an analysis of these innovative geniuses, the authors built a survey focused on the five emergent innovative skills that trigger innovative thinking to deliver new businesses, products, services, or processes; all innovators engage in these regularly:

1. **Questioning:** Innovators constantly question the status quo. Every high-profile innovative entrepreneur in the study scored above the 70th percentile in questioning and associating.

2. **Observing**: Innovators are also intense observers. They watch the world around them, including customers, products, services, technologies, and companies. Such observations help them gain a sense of perspective and vision.

3. **Networking**: Innovators spend a lot of energy finding and testing ideas through a diverse network of individuals with very different backgrounds and perspectives. Innovative networkers search for new ideas by talking to people with different views.

4. **Experimenting**: Innovators are constantly experimenting with new experiences and piloting new ideas. Experimenters unceasingly explore the world intellectually and experientially by holding convictions at bay and testing hypotheses along the way.

5. **Associating**: Questioning, observing, networking, and experimenting all lead to associative thinking. The cognitive skill of the brain to take in new information, relate it to something else already in the brain, and create something new is called associating.

## What Innovative Leaders Can Do

To generate creative-innovative DNA, innovative leaders can:

- Create a climate that questions the status quo as a regular process. Build in meeting time for people to challenge "what is" with what "could be." Allow "what if" questions or what would happen when we combined A with B. The tougher the questions allowed, the more likely the potential for innovation.

- Allow time for people to observe, think, and wonder; give them the space to create. Especially expose people to customers using your product or service. Observing how customers use and understand why they "hired" the widget, cup of coffee, or piece of software opens creativity doors wider and wider.

- Push all employees to get out, network, and interact with diverse networks of consumers, colleagues, and crowds that they're not used to hanging out with. Let them attend conferences and symposia in fields much different from their own. Such loosely connected groups can have a profound effect on products and services because their eyes are fresh, honest, and diverse.

- Let people test, observe, and modify. Becoming experimental pushes ideas and products from the status quo to something bright, new, and re-adapted. Think about the Google and Apple mindsets focused on "letting go of the status quo."
- Encourage variant thinking. Push people to take in new information (by questioning, networking, and by being open and experimental).

Here's what innovative leaders can do to help personality types work together creatively:

- Recognize that people have fundamental and amazing differences.
- Celebrate and use those differences to build a better mousetrap.
- Understand that Sensors are tactical, and Intuitors are strategic.
- Partner Sensors with Intuitors, and you have the formula for creativity and execution—the spark for the creativity-to-innovation path.
- Make sure that for every Intuitor you have at least three to five Sensors to actually execute on the big, important ideas.
- Understand that creativity only happens with diversity. People thinking differently with diverse backgrounds and perspectives generate new thought.

# Engagement

The Gallup organization has used its ability to research and analyze mountains of data related to people and teams to produce a book, *Strengths Based Leadership: Great Leaders, Teams, and Why People Follow*, worthy of any team or organization reading it. These are the basic premises:

- People perform best when they're engaged in their work.
- Engagement only happens when people work in their strengths areas—what they're best at.

Individuals may not be well-rounded or possess strengths in all areas—a virtual impossibility. However, based on extensive Gallup research, teams need to be well-balanced across four key domains: execution, influence, relationship building, and strategic thinking. Further, there are 34 StrengthsFinder talent themes that become true strengths when used and practiced—like any skill—and these talent themes are further sorted out into nearly equal sets of the four key domains. To remember the four domains, think of the word SIRE.

- **Strategic thinking**: People with developed strengths in this domain tend to force the group to look at the big picture and toward the future—what might be. Always reviewing the data and applying what they learn, strategic thinkers move the organization forward—stretching its members to think beyond what is, to the possibilities of the future.
- **Influence**: People with developed strengths in this key domain know how to sell or promulgate the team's ideas both inside and outside the organization. These people are natural persuaders, inspire others to adopt their ideas, and are vital to moving teams forward in communities.
- **Relationship building**: Those with developed strengths in this domain tend to keep groups together. They're the social glue, the mortar between the foundation building blocks. They know how to create and maintain groups such that the whole is much greater than its parts.
- **Execution**: People with developed strengths in this key domain know how to rally around a goal and get things done. Differing strengths might dictate the style of getting to the goal, but folks who have strengths in this domain area contribute mightily to execution.

When individuals take StrengthsFinder, if two or more of the 34 talent themes are found under a given SIRE domain, consider customizing that person's job to take advantage of those talents—especially if they've developed them into strengths. Also offer opportunities and training to develop those talent themes into true strengths.

Gallup conducted more than 20,000 in-depth interviews, studied more than 1 million work teams, considered more than 50 years of data on the world's most admired leaders, and studied more than 10,000 followers for insights into leaders. Here's what that data revealed:

- The most effective leaders are always investing in strengths.
- Employees who do not work in strengths areas are only 9 percent engaged in their jobs, compared with 74 percent engagement levels for people who do work in their strengths. Further, engagement has been proven to substantially increase productivity for the company.
- Engaged employees produce roughly 30 percent more than others.
- The most effective leaders surround themselves with the right complementary people and then maximize their teams.
- By nature, we all have talents that can be developed into strengths. We also have definite weaknesses. And while no leader is perfectly well rounded, effective teams must be well rounded to perform at a high level.

# Mindset

What's the difference between failing and learning? Your mindset! According to Carol Dweck, famed Stanford psychologist, in her book *Mindset: The New Psychology of Success*, it all boils down to whether you think of talent or intelligence as either a fixed ability or one capable of growth through effort and practice. Often it comes down to whether you seek validation or a challenge. If you view the world through the fixed mindset window or through a growth mindset, it will definitely color your future.

## Fixed Mindset

Fixed-mindset people try to prove themselves and support their self-image of success. This leads them to try to "look smart," constantly building an image, even putting others down to preserve their personal standing. All encounters become matters of success or failure, looking smart or stupid, being accepted or rejected, or feeling like a winner or a loser. Such a fixed orientation makes people avoid risk, stop learning and experimenting, and be defensive. Such a mindset is anathema to creativity and thus, to innovation. Eventually these behaviors cause such people to fall behind competitors and become less relevant—the very thing they are trying to avoid.

Fixed-mindset people aspire to "effortless perfection." They think that only people who are not perfect or smart need to work to succeed. They disdain effort because they see it as a risk and a potential for failure.

Fixed mindsets also want to validate their status and act like superstars, afraid to just be a team member. Dweck refers to the somebody-nobody syndrome: "If I win, I'll be somebody; if I lose, I'll be nobody."

## Growth Mindset

Growth-mindset people don't believe that they're stuck with the hand they were dealt. Rather, they believe that you get better with practice and that you can cultivate qualities through effort and engagement. This attitude creates a real thirst for knowledge, as opposed to being recognized merely as smart or intelligent. Those with growth mindsets will eschew looking smart in favor of truly learning and getting better. They stretch themselves, confront challenges, and take risks rather than playing it safe; thus they open up new and exciting doors. Growth-mindset people get their motivation from trying and learning. They see setbacks as wake-up calls and motivational grist for future improvement, and they take charge of success processes. Creative people like to test and probe even if they experience failure along the way as long as they're learning and discovering.

To foster creativity and a growth mindset, we should all avoid telling people—especially our own children—that they're so smart or intelligent. Such remarks make them want to live in a perfectionist, fixed mindset. A fixed mindset makes them want to stay within their current "reputation" and not take chances that might show they're not always so smart. People will not try to create while in a fixed mindset because of a fear of not looking smart. For example, in an academic world, fixed-mindset students won't take challenging courses and are even more likely to cheat to maintain their status of being smart.

Instead, we should compliment people—especially children—on their hard work and perseverance. Noticing their hard work encourages them to experiment, try, fail, and try again. Such experimentation is the mantra of great entrepreneurs. Perseverance also opens the door for acceptable mistakes, a lack of perfection, and a way of continually trying and experimenting.

Try celebrating failure. This is important because failure discovers what does not work. No inventor would have made any discovery without failing first. Failure is always an important option, not a disgrace. Encourage risk taking, not needless or reckless risk taking, but sensible and curious-driven risk.

Discourage perfection—unless your business is packing parachutes!

Talented people, allowed to be creative and experimental, can produce the level and kind of creative thought that changes the world—especially if there exists an environment that allows such creative thought to spawn.

In the next installment of our story, Roland Epps's detective agency continues to evolve, as the former police detective now small business entrepreneur begins to gather the talent he needs for a first-class investigative organization.

# THE STORY: The Team of Differences

Over their first year of operation, the detectives at Epps Security continued their busy pace, and when they were able to make a couple key hires in the midst of the steady flow of cases demanding their attention, they felt relieved and self-congratulatory. Now, only because of the regular office presence of their new office manager, Jenn, and Dan, a forensics accountant, Roland and Bill were able to take a spring afternoon off with Dana for a ballgame at Washington Nationals Park. But make no mistake, this was a work outing—thinly disguised as a day at the ballpark.

The partners could agree on one thing: the first year of business had flown by. But was it like an opposite-field homer—a ferocious sustained smacking shot, direct and on the money—or more like a soft flare into the no-man's land of center to bring in the runner from third—and be just as effective? Which was their trajectory, their business model? This Roland and Bill debated as they sat along the third-base line on the rare occasion of a Nats-Orioles late afternoon game in early May.

The season was young, with possibilities stretching out for both teams—just like the two partners—a great time to be a fan, or in a young, thriving business. The bottom line, they agreed, was that they were pleased with the agency's growth and prosperity.

Dana, however, seated between the two, was keeping them on their toes. "Isn't this the reason you asked me to meet you? To help clarify these differences?"

Their business was growing rapidly and even with the addition of the two new employees, they could not keep up the kind of continuity their customers wanted.

"We need to add capacity if we're going to step up our game," said Bill.

"I agree," Dana said. "Talent is the cornerstone of the Innovation Equation." She had explained the Innovation Equation (Innovation = Talent + Environment + Process) during the drive to the park and now went on to explain that talent had three elements to consider: cognitive diversity, engagement, and mindset.

"First and foremost you need cognitive diversity—people thinking differently to solve problems by having different ways of looking at the same problem. So, tell me about your team," she said.

"Last winter we added a forensics specialist and a computer tech," said Roland. "They're curious and excited to be part of a young business, and we expect them to not mind wearing lots of hats."

Suddenly, a crack of the bat and everyone leaned forward to follow a long fly ball headed for the centerfield fence. Dana groaned with the rest of the crowd as the ball hung up in the cool air to be caught, leaving the bases loaded with Nats. She took a long swallow of her beer. "I'm buying dinner after the game so you guys can tell me about the personalities of your team," she said.

Leaving the park after the game, which the Nats pulled out in spite of putting three O's on base with no outs in the ninth and wild pitching a run in ("Ah spring!" exclaimed Roland), the detective's thoughts turned to his own team. He knew the most about their personalities and began to describe them to Dana.

"Dan's big and quiet. Great with detail, logical, and delivers on time, every time." As Roland talked, he steered the group up 8th Street toward his favorite Italian restaurant near Nats Park, Lavagna.

Minutes later they were seated at a sidewalk table, enjoying the spring night, and Dana began to sketch out letters on a piece of paper, using her favorite black felt-tipped pen.

As Roland talked, Dana asked questions: "Can you give me an example? What do you mean by Jenn's mostly verbal?"

When Roland was done, Dana nodded, doodled a bit more with the letters she was placing next to people's names on the paper napkin. Finally, Roland asked, "So what's the verdict? What'd you come up with?"

Dana juggled some notes and letters a bit more and then nodded to the list as a kind of affirmation that she was good with what she came up with. She then looked up and said: "Look, these are just my back-of-the-envelope assessments of your crew. To get more accuracy, you really may want to get them to take the Myers-Briggs Type Indicator." Then she explained the two new members of the team to Roland and Bill. Here's the summary of Dana's notes:

- DAN—LARGE, MUSCULAR, TATTOOED EX-MARINE CORPS—IS LIKELY AN ISTJ (A MILITARY MAN): INTROVERTED (GETS ENERGY FROM BEING ALONE); SENSORY (GOOD WITH DETAIL AND DATA); THINKER (LOGICAL DECISION MAKER); JUDGER (A GOOD CLOSER).
- JENN—NATURAL-BORN MANAGER OR TEACHER WITH A TATTOO ON HER LEFT CALF OF A LIGHTNING BOLT—IS AN ESTJ (TAKE-CHARGE TYPE): SOCIAL, HONEST, RESPONSIBLE; EXTROVERTED; SENSOR; THINKER; JUDGER.

"And don't forget our new medical researcher, Rachel," Roland added, turning toward his partner. "I know we said temp through the summer, but don't you think we need her pharmacological background?"

Bill turned to smile at Dana across the table. "I think I'm the one who wanted to hire her in the first place, so, yes, let's add Rachel."

- RACHEL—QUIET, CHEERFUL FRIEND OF JENN, WHO CAME BY TO PICK HER UP FOR DINNER ONE MARCH EVENING—IS AN ISFP (A PLEASER AND CHANCE TAKER): INTERESTED IN MEDICAL WRITING AS A CAREER; INTROVERTED; SENSOR; FEELER; PERCEIVER.

"Wow, that's a pretty interesting mix," Bill said.

"Doubt you could have gotten a more diverse mix if you'd tried," Dana said, "and as for you guys—Roland's an ENFP—a born actor, teacher, entrepreneur."

"And, Bill, of course, you're an ISTJ," Dana said smiling.

Bill looked at his team list and said, "Yep, always knew I liked Dan!"

"So, Dana, what's it all mean to our business?" Roland asked.

Dana went on to explain that when creating a team, diversity of personality always helps because it gives you a diverse "worldview," another set of eyes to look at the situation from varying perspectives.

"You tend to make better, more balanced decisions, if and when no single personality is allowed to dominate the group, otherwise you get into 'groupthink'—everyone agreeing to a reality they may not really believe in—just to conform."

"Yeah, like when the chief used to push us to charge and arrest perps to get the reporters off our backs!" Roland said looking right at Bill, "You remember the Henderson case."

"All too well," said Bill.

"The Henderson case?" Dana asked, "Explain, please."

So Roland ordered coffee and tiramisu for three and then began to tell the story of local real estate agent Jack Henderson, who had a reputation for the high life along with a new wife.

Roland started: "Well, Dana, as George V. Higgins might say, Jack was the 'classiest sleazy' real estate agent around. Just a simple guy with rich tastes. Fast cars, expensive suits. . . ."

Bill interjected, "Jack coulda fooled anyone," leaning back in his chair. "He seemed a successful, busy, social guy. Ran a small residential real estate franchise for his father, finally married."

"The new wife was beautiful, refined, and smart," added Roland. "You could say their social circles didn't really mesh. They met when he sold her a house."

"She was well known," Bill said admiringly, "a local public radio personality with a great voice, late-afternoon drive-time show, and she also did a lot of philanthropy."

"Jack had been seen around with another client, a nurse, and there was talk about them," said Roland. "The thing was, the nurse was married, with a couple kids, and Jack with no children didn't seem the father type."

"So what did Jack do?" asked Dana impatiently. "What was his crime?"

The two partners looked at each other, then at Dana, and spoke almost in unison, "Fell in love."

"The thing was this," said Roland, in his best case-summarizing tone, holding a forkful of tiramisu aloft: "One day the wife disappears, but Jack never reports her missing. Friends and co-workers call. Nothing. So, where is she? Jack doesn't appear to have a clue. And does he seem upset? Not much."

"But the press was pushing the chief for information," said Bill, "and he was pushing the investigating team—especially Roland—to present a case to the prosecutor. Much to the chief's dismay, Roland held off."

Roland added: "You can't prosecute somebody just because you don't like him, and the chief didn't like Jack. He had a grudge, pure and simple. There'd been a housing loan scam a few years earlier that he'd not been able to get Jack on, but this was . . ."

"Murder?" Dana interjected.

"But there was no case!" Roland shot back. "No body! Just suspicions and suspicious behavior."

"But the other thing was," Roland continued, leaning forward in his best confiding tone, "the wife had a much-loved dog, a prizewinning French barbet named Camus, and that dog was not to be found. A leash and maybe biscuits but no dog."

"Isn't it always the case? Breadcrumbs, dog biscuits, all the same," said Dana, crossing her arms in front of her and shaking her head.

"It's a rare breed," said Roland matter-of-factly. "French water dog. Lots of fur in the face, long woolly coat, quite beautiful actually. Not every dog in the park."

"So Roland figures—find the dog and find the wife," said Bill.

"And bingo! Took almost a year, but eventually I went to enough shows with enough water dogs that I flushed her out. Found her in upstate New York, if you can believe it, beautiful little town near the Canadian border, putting Camus through his paces around the ring. So focused on the dog, she didn't see me push into the front row right in front of her."

"What could you say? She committed no crime," Dana said.

"That's right," Roland agreed. "The crime of what, indifference to anyone who cared about her?"

"Except for Jack," said Dana sadly.

Roland turned to her and smiled. "Turns out Jack really did love the nurse; they'd been college sweethearts and hadn't been able to forget each other."

"Families came between them," explained Bill.

"Well, his," said Roland. "Country club set, investment bankers, took a dive during the recession."

"So not a cad after all, least of all," said Dana.

"Maybe guilty . . . of a character flaw," said Roland. "Not marrying the nurse first really was his youthful undoing, if you can believe that. He told me he wasted years. Never recovered from the fallout with his family, never ventured out with his own business. Grew somewhat bitter and resentful."

"But then the nurse had a personal crisis," added Bill, "very sick kid, looming divorce, money problems. Suddenly Jack feels he's been living a lie. When he finally comes clean and confesses to his wife, she splits, leaving Jack to deal on his own. He couldn't get over the first love."

"Listen to you guys, such romantics," said Dana.

"The wife wasn't being vindictive," said Roland. "She told me she just wanted to take some time, to get away and think, but she panicked when she saw all the news reports and gossip and decided to just lay low. Follow the dog show circuit for a while."

"Love is merely a madness," Dana said staring into her coffee cup. "And time the scarcest thing of all. Unless it's managed, nothing else can be managed."

The partners looked from each other to Dana.

"Shakespeare . . . and Peter Drucker," she said.

"The chief eventually thanked me, but secretly I think he resented that it took so long to solve and would have preferred me pinning something on Jack anyway!" Roland said.

"Now I remember her!" Dana suddenly exclaimed. "The Case of the Stray Barbet!"

"It ended OK," Bill said. "Jack finally married the nurse, and I think Camus won a show or two. Everyone's happy."

"Yep, some are extroverted, others introverted—and still others are just plain nuts!" Roland laughed.

## Roland's Notes

- [ ] INNOVATION = TALENT + ENVIRONMENT + PROCESS.
- [ ] MOTIVATION IS ABOUT SATISFACTION; IT'S SOCIAL AND PURPOSE DRIVEN.
- [ ] WHAT'S THE DIFFERENCE BETWEEN FAILING AND LEARNING?
- [ ] COGNITIVE DIVERSITY: PEOPLE WITH DIFFERENT VIEWS OF THE SAME PROBLEM.
- [ ] AVOID SOMEBODY—NOBODY SYNDROME.
- [ ] FAILURE IS AN OPTION, NOT A DISGRACE.
- [ ] DISCOURAGE PERFECTION.
- [ ] GROWTH—MINDSET PEOPLE DON'T BELIEVE THEY'RE STUCK WITH THE HAND THEY WERE DEALT. (JACK!)

# References

Dweck, C. 2006. *Mindset: The New Psychology of Success.* New York: Random House.

Dyer, J., H. Gregersen, and C.M. Christensen. 2011. *The Innovator's DNA: Mastering the Five Skills of Disruptive Innovators.* Boston: Harvard Business Review Press.

——. 2009. "The Innovator's DNA." *Harvard Business Review*, December.

Gladis, S.D. 1993. *Writetype: Personality Types and Writing Styles*. Amherst, MA: HRD Press.

Jung, C.G. 1990. *Psychological Types: The Collected Works of C.G. Jung*. Vol. 6. Princeton, NJ: Princeton University Press.

Rath, T., and B. Conchie. 2013. *Strengths Based Leadership: Great Leaders, Teams, and Why People Follow*. New York: Gallup Press.

Simmons, J., and A. Corso. 2013. *Letting Go of the Status Quo: The Liberating, Exhilarating Journey of Two Women Who Reinvented Themselves and Your Guide to Do the Same*. Dallastown, PA: Love Your Life Publishing.

# 3

# THE INNOVATION EQUATION
# PART 2: ENVIRONMENT

To nurture creative talent, leaders need to develop a sustaining environment—an intentional culture of motivation. For people to be creative and for teams and organizations—companies, nonprofits, and government agencies—to be innovative, certain cultural "ecological" conditions have to exist to allow creativity to thrive. Thus, if creativity is the seed, then motivation is one key element in the soil that cultivates, nurtures, and grows creativity into full-blooming innovation. Interestingly, after World War II, two American psychologists, Abraham Maslow and Frederick Herzberg, developed motivational models that helped cut through the data and provide great insights into developing the supportive culture for the innovative process to happen.

## Maslow's Hierarchy of Needs

According to Maslow's now iconic hierarchy of needs, human needs are ranked, and certain ones, such as physiological (water, food, and air) and safety, must be met before ascending the ladder to more lofty endeavors, such as belonging, esteem, and self-actualization or fulfillment (Figure 3-1). People tend to be creative when they reach a state of self-actualization. Moreover, Maslow believed that we should focus on people's positive qualities rather than what's wrong with them.

## Figure 3-1: Maslow's Hierarchy of Needs

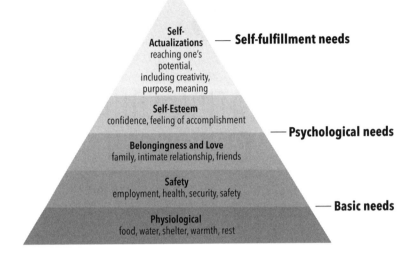

# Herzberg's Two-Factor Theory

Following Maslow, Herzberg developed his two-factor theory, also called the Motivation Hygiene Theory, which maps to Maslow's hierarchy of needs, with some differences (Figure 3-2). Herzberg's now famous article, "One More Time: How Do You Motivate Employees?" published in the *Harvard Business Review*, is one of the most read articles in the publication's history. Herzberg studied accountants and engineers about what satisfied and motivated them in their jobs. In a nutshell, this is what he found: Job satisfaction and job motivation were two different things, which he called hygiene and motivation. What satisfied people, he called "hygiene" factors. We might call these satisfiers employee needs, such as salary, benefits, vacation, healthcare, and a 401k plan. Other satisfiers that constitute hygiene include management practices, such as policies, supervision, and work conditions; relationships with the boss, peers, and direct reports; and status and security. Also called extrinsic incentives,"these hygiene satisfiers are outside the work itself; they attract people to the job, even keep them there a while, but they don't retain people for the long haul. Bottom line: People need their hygiene factors taken care of to satisfy them. If dissatisfied, they will not be productive, let alone creative, and will likely leave their jobs at the first opportunity.

## Figure 3-2: Herzberg's Motivation Hygiene Theory

**Motivational Factors**
Interesting, challenging work
Use of one's capabilities
Opportunity to do something meaningful
Recognition
Advancement
Access to information
Responsibility

**Hygiene Maintenance Factors**
Relations with co-workers
Working conditions
Pensions
Paid insurance
Job security
Vacations
Holidays
Salary

However, to engage workers meaningfully, even when they're not at work, it takes much more than satisfiers. Herzberg called these sustaining factors "motivators." Also called intrinsic rewards, such motivating factors are all about the work itself. These motivators include work that fits a person's strengths, recognition for achievement, opportunity to do meaningful work, and engagement in decision making—all related to an employee's direct relationship to the work itself and engagement with the company's progress. Company cultures that foster these intrinsic, motivating factors retain employees, increase productivity, and stay at the top of their industry. Those that don't weaken, falter, and fail.

# The Motivation Pyramid

Positioned between the research of Maslow and Herzberg, I propose a derivative model: the Motivation Pyramid (Figure 3-3). The essential premise of this model is that people have to feel supported on three important levels: satisfaction, social, and purpose.

Figure 3-3: The Motivation Pyramid

To foster creativity, leaders must first establish an environment, an intentional culture, which provides employees with what they need (satisfaction), so that they are not focused solely on basic survival. Thus, pay must be adequate—neither at the poverty level nor at the highest pay scales. In fact, only after fundamental needs are met in terms of salary, healthcare, job security, vacation, good working conditions, a decent boss, and other important benefits are people likely to get creative. Otherwise, they use all their creative energy just to keep their heads above water—playing defense. Thus, satisfaction is the foundation for the Motivation Pyramid onto which two other key elements (social and purpose) rest.

Next, humans are fundamentally wired to be social and to connect. We are pack animals. Neuroscientist and psychologist Matthew Lieberman explains in *Social: Why Our Brains Are Wired to Connect* just how social we are from birth to death and how our very health depends on connecting with others in ways that are intimate and meaningful. In *Social Physics: How Good Ideas Spread—The Lessons From a New Science*, Alex Pentland of MIT describes how the new ways of collecting big data relate to social connections and can more fully explain human social behavior in our "hyperconnected, networked society." Pentland's extensive data collection method using electronic badges worn by participants on the job accurately measures how we act socially by recording how often, with whom, how long, and other patterns of interaction we engage in. Thus, social sits mid-level in the Motivation Pyramid, atop satisfaction, serving as the transition between surviving and thriving.

Finally, people need a strong sense of purpose at work. There seems to be no doubt that intrinsic stimulation—motivation, inspiration, engagement, and focus on a purpose make all the difference between low and high performers, whether on a playing field or at work. Moreover, when it comes to work, we now know through the research of Teresa Amabile and Steven Kramer, offered in their book, *The Progress Principle: Using Small Wins to Ignite Joy, Engagement, and Creativity at Work,* that people simply want to make progress toward meaningful work every day—striving toward progress. Leaders who facilitate purposeful work will be seen as good leaders and those who do not will be seen as poor leaders—creating frustration and personnel turnover. Thus, purpose sits at the very top of the Motivation Pyramid.

## The Motivation Matrix

While understanding that the Motivation Pyramid is critical, further understanding about how the pyramid applies not only to individuals but also to teams and organizations unlocks the power of the Motivation Matrix (Table 3-1). Such application across the organization creates a default innovative culture—a way of doing things—that can transform a great idea into an innovative product or service that gets sold on the market.

Table 3-1: The Motivation Matrix

| The Motivation Pyramid | People | Teams | Organizations |
|---|---|---|---|
| *Purpose* | Purpose Driven | Mission Focused | Vision Centric |
| *Social* | Socially Connected | Socially Collaborative | Culturally Integrated |
| *Satisfaction* | Needs Met | Team Supported | Organizationally Stable |

To find practical ways to foster a culture of creativity for individuals, it's worth referring to the Motivation Matrix. Note that people, teams, and organizations have to feel satisfied and very safe before they can begin to think about getting socially connected. And only then do they get stimulated—motivated to take risks, stick out their necks, and try something really creative.

# What Innovative Leaders Can Do for People

Here are some practical things leaders can do to support people becoming more creative.

## Satisfy Basic Needs

At a basic level, innovative leaders need to pay a decent wage—figure out what the market salary rate is and pay it. Going cheap is as bad as overpaying. They're flip sides of the same coin—don't under- or overpay. People want to work for good leaders and do important, meaningful things. They just don't want to be taken advantage of. Nor do they ultimately want to be overpaid; it makes them feel unfair or dishonest.

Next, leaders must provide market benefits to take care of people's families; employees need healthcare, a path to retirement (eventually), time off to enjoy with their families and get a break from work—and a range of benefits reasonably expected for the culture and context in which they live. Benefits might differ for both the industry and location, so leaders need to figure out the context and location and provide accordingly.

Innovative leaders should ensure excellent working conditions. People want to work at a decent place, with decent people, and for a decent leader. Providing the equipment (computer, desk, and space); decent, caring colleagues (comparably educated and trained, competent, and caring); and a leader whom they can trust, respect, and who supports them sets the stage—the culture for future success.

Having met basic satisfaction needs, innovative leaders can address the social needs of their employees by modeling good behavior. Common sense and research supports this notion (Kouzes and Posner 2012). People watch what leaders do, and if it matches what they say—the say-do continuum—they are more likely to do the same. Any inconsistent leadership behavior, and people will be confused and believe a leader's actions over their words—every time.

Treat people like valued treasure: The Golden Rule is "Do unto others as you would have them do to you." I have modified that statement into the Golden Rule Squared for Leaders: "Do unto others as you would have them do to your children." We treasure nothing more dearly than our children and adopting that same mindset—not a paternalistic or materialistic view but leading from a sense of true well-meaning—creates a workplace that few will leave. There is ample research to support the fact that people leave managers not jobs (Cashman 2008). Be the leader you'd want your son or daughter to work for.

## Be Welcoming

Onboard individuals to the team. Most people are extroverted and like to work on teams. And while there are birds who like to fly alone, most prefer flocks. Creating a good flock is a leader's job. And that takes diligence and effort. Leaders must create ways to effectively onboard people to the organization. Take time, invest energy, and pay attention to do this properly when new employees come aboard, or suffer the consequence of costly turnovers. Properly onboarded employees are more creative and effective much sooner than people just tossed into the deep waters of established teams. The first day at work is like the first day at school. Make it welcoming and see the difference it makes.

## Nurture Strengths and Support Progress

Everyone wants to matter—that their life counts for something. A sense of purpose in life is the ultimate goal for people. Progress toward a meaningful goal every day drives many of us. Innovative leaders can make purpose and meaning happen when they nurture strengths. For example, find out what people are good at and help them become great at it. Determine what's in their heart—why they like to do what they do—the core of their purpose. It might be creativity, service, or being part of something bigger. Then, give them opportunity and support to do what they do best and apply it to their jobs. If someone is good at writing, find a way to craft their job toward that very strength. Much has been written on how to actively employ "job crafting" for employees (Berg, Dutton, and Wrzesniewski 2007). Job crafting involves shifting overall team responsibilities throughout the team based on people's strengths—allowing employees to spend more time doing what they're good at.

Next, leaders should be sure to support progress. For example, become a catalyst, not an impediment, to progress—for people and teams. The path is simple: Remove barriers and provide support. To the extent that managers facilitate progress they'll be viewed as valued leaders. To the extent they're viewed as barriers to progress, they'll be viewed as impediments to progress and as bad leaders (Amabile and Kramer 2011).

Finally, trust people. Leaders do well by giving people the autonomy to do what they do well every day and trusting them to do the right thing. Instead of monitoring them, or catching them doing the wrong things, catch them doing the right things—then compliment them in public. Note that if, as a leader, you want trust from employees, give them trust first. That's how reciprocity, a very powerful influencer, works (Cialdini 2006).

## What Innovative Leaders Can Do for Teams

To find practical ways to foster creativity-to-innovation for teams, refer to the Motivation Matrix. For teams to be motivated and scale to innovation, they must be fully supported, the people and team need to be socially collaborative, and the team must be mission centric. One could hardly envision a Super Bowl team that was not fully supported, socially collaborative, or mission centric. But no matter the scale—whether it's a company softball team, the kitchen crew at your local diner, or the warehouse staff at your favorite garden-supply store—good teams can make an organization successful.

Teams are essential to scale a creative idea to the next level. Leaders can help by first supporting basic needs, such as getting proper funding. Teams cost money. They can be productive, creative, can turn a company from unprofitable to profitable, and they require proper, dedicated, and long-term funding for success. No money, no mission. No innovation, no company.

## Fully Supported: Get Commitment

Innovative leaders need to get commitment from many critical people in the organization to understand and support the team's mission. Often, sacrifice is required from varying elements in the company to stand up a new team or focus a standing team on an emerging innovation. Stakeholder support from peers, leaders, and direct reports is essential for the innovative team to thrive.

Teams also need resources—people (talent), materials, and especially a place to be a team. Even virtual teams need a place to hang out—a good electronic platform. The idea of group genius comes from the ability of team members to intellectually rub up against each other. This comes from well-designed space that captures the needs of the project and the personality of the group. Common areas, chat rooms, maker spaces, and areas of casual collaboration make the magic of teams "happen."

## Socially Collaborative: Ensure Team Balance and Voice

Having met these basic requirements, innovative leaders next need to ensure that social needs are addressed. The power of teams results from harnessing and respecting their individual differences—especially their cognitive differences—how they think differently about the same thing. Like the old children's story "Stone Soup," everyone brings their individual, differing ingredients (gifts) to the pot and when allowed to simmer together, they make a wonderful soup.

Every new person whom a leader adds to the team creates a potential benefit and change. And change can also represent a threat; so, add people carefully and thoughtfully. Allowing team members to have a voice in the selection and having decent onboarding processes can ensure a much greater chance of success for new team members.

## Mission Centric: Create Mission Focus

Focusing on something bigger than themselves helps strong-willed, talented team members keep their eyes on what matters most: the team mission. Innovative leaders make the mission central when they create focus. Leaders unite organizations with a clear, well-articulated focus.

U.S. Marines put it this way: "The main thing is to keep the main thing the main thing!" People want to make progress toward a meaningful goal. To do that, they need to focus on necessary goals, which agree not only with their personal objectives but also with larger and more unifying mission objectives. Innovative leaders paint a clear picture of what things will look like if the entire team works together. Focus is a day-by-day issue that innovative leaders deal with to help teams stay on track.

Often, leaders focus so much on the bottom line that they push their teams from one victory to the next, never taking time to celebrate and savor every win. In a similar but very different way, leaders need to accept and learn from losses, both personal and professional, with their teams but not ruminate over them.

Be intentional to incentivize teams over people. Team effort and interdependence take creativity to the next level—innovation. Only interdependent teams and eventually an organization have the power to take a creative idea to full-blown innovation, so emphasize team goals and accomplishments to drive home the advantage that teams have on innovation.

# What Innovative Leaders Can Do for Organizations

To find practical ways to foster creativity-to-innovation for organizations, refer again to the Motivation Matrix. Note that people, teams, and organizations have to feel a sense of satisfaction before they can begin to think about getting social and collaborating. And only then can an organization become stimulated enough to launch an innovative product or process.

## Be Organizationally Stable

Think about any successful, adaptive organization—for example, IBM adapting to technological change; the Red Cross adapting to crisis; even your neighborhood coffee shop tweaking that special blend that you now prefer to the popular chain's brew; or your dry cleaner offering 24/7 pick-up and drop-off technology—you'll find an innovative organization at work.

## Get Leadership Straight

Innovative leaders set the tone, the atmosphere, and the culture for organizational innovation by ensuring that their entities are organizationally stable, culturally integrated, and vision focused.

Stability in any organization starts with the leader (CEO) and moves throughout the organization. Focus on hiring and promoting the best. Never be afraid to surround yourself with people smarter than you—that shows you're the smart one! Establish rigorous processes to recruit, train, and retain good leaders. It all starts with stable leadership.

## Get Finances Straight

Next, organizations require long-term, strategic investment. Innovation isn't cheap and requires experimentation, failure, discovery—and that requires long-term financial backing. At different stages of development, organizations focus on different funding models. Early-stage companies have "angel investors," a kind of friends-and-family support. But as organizations expand and need greater funding sources, they may pursue venture capital or stock ownership. But whatever the financial model, it's good to remember: No money, no mission, no innovation, no future company. Big innovative projects require forward vision, courage, and substantial financial resources. An unfinanced vision is like a bridge halfway across a river—better known as a diving board (Rowley 2014).

## Stand Up a Dedicated Team

Pulling together an innovation team, a dedicated team (Govindarajan 2010), requires both investment and commitment from the main business that will have to support and nurture this new bet (Sims 2011) in the future. That requires CEOs and other executive leaders to persuade insiders to support the dedicated team, or it will fail. The leader of the new dedicated team also must have the support and confidence of the people in the main line of the business to keep the support coming, especially when there are necessary experiments that can and will fail along the way.

# Be Culturally Integrated

Having met basic organizational needs, cultural integration becomes essential for larger organizations.

## Respect Culture

To do this, innovative leaders need to respect culture. According to culture guru Edgar Schein, "Culture is about learned group behaviors to solve problems in the external environment to ensure internal integration, stability, consistency and meaning—those things worthy of teaching to new team members as the 'correct' way to think and act toward solving similar problems." Culture relates to a group the same way as personality does to a person. Just as personal norms dictate our behavior, group norms (culture) dictate how groups behave. Culture change is all about a threat-reward stimulus, learning, and adapting to survive. If learning new ways (change) creates more anxiety than solves problems, people will balk. Culture boils down to artifacts, espoused beliefs, and basic assumptions. Leaders make or break change in organizations. Understanding and respecting culture before trying to change it is essential for innovation. Deserving special note here is the culture-development work of Kim Cameron and Robert Quinn at the University of Michigan. They developed the Competing Values Framework, describing organizations as having elements of four competing sets of values: Clan (focused on collaboration and human development); Adhocracy (focused on creativity and change); Market (focused on competition and customers); and Hierarchy (focused on control and process).

## Build Solid, Culturally Connected Teams

Teams and their leaders have to be culturally connected to each other and not be allowed to operate in independent silos—despite subcultures that each team will naturally develop. Rather, those silos—team cultures—have to be connected and subservient to the larger corporate culture; otherwise, the magic of integration never happens. Teams get best integrated by working toward a participative vision-focused goal that they have a hand in crafting.

# Be Vision Focused

When organizations are stable and culture is integrated, effective leaders get everyone focused on a corporate vision—an innovative product or service. Such a vision is a statement of hope about the future state of a product or service that will influence and motivate people and teams to seek that vision with passion.

## Develop a Collective Vision

Every new organization starts with a vision—a hope in the unseen future. An innovative leader who—with the help and input of those around him or her—is willing to peer into the future and see what a new corporate product or service could be, gives the organization a primal element: a target to focus on. Next, for leaders to calibrate their vision, they will want to validate it by asking stakeholders (potential customers and partners) inside and outside the company for their insights. Then, a collective vision has to be negotiated. Gone are the days of a leader pointing to an objective and having everyone salute and fall in line. Finally, leaders have to sell that collective vision up and down, inside and outside the organization using influence and inspiration.

## Develop a Strategy

A vision without a plan for execution is a form of delusion. Strategy is a plan to get to a vision or goal. It's the story about how you'll get from the current state to the desired future state (vision). No strategy is like having no money. No strategy, no vision achieved. Oftentimes, strategies get overly complex and convoluted such that virtually no one knows which direction to push toward. Keep it simple and comprehensible, so that everyone in the company can draw a picture of it on a yellow sticky note and say, "That's our strategy," with pride.

## Monitor, Recalibrate, Celebrate

"What doesn't get measured, doesn't get done!" Everyone's likely heard that old maxim—usually from an accountant—at some time or other! But when it comes to vision and strategy, monitoring the results quarter to quarter and year to year makes great sense. Good leaders demand systematic reporting—with regular demands of all to explain their progress toward the strategy and the corporate vision. One word of caution, getting too hung up on quarter-to-quarter results hurts companies with long-term vision. Leaders should be careful not to allow the short term to destroy the long-term vision.

Market conditions change all the time. And when change happens, like a good quarterback calling an audible at the line of scrimmage, an innovative leader needs to adapt and recalibrate the vision expectations. Such recalibration needs to be done with care—neither too fast, nor too slow. The art comes in knowing when to make a shift and how big a shift to make.

Importantly, when teams and organizations reach collective goals, even interim ones, leaders need to know how to celebrate. Taking time to celebrate along the way keeps people energized and inspired. Not false celebration, but real, genuine goal-focused celebration keeps the company recharged and ready to move forward.

Creative talent is not enough to make innovation happen. Talent serves as the seed, which requires the right soil in which to be planted, and a motivational environment provides such soil to grow innovation.

What did our two private detectives, recently retired, know about soil and environment? Only that they were about to get their hands dirty.

## THE STORY: The Motivation Matrix

Roland stood in the doorway soaking wet, head to toe, and shook like a dog until he got Jenn's attention.

"Just a summer shower, boss," she said, glancing up from her computer before thunder boomed through the bank of double-hung windows behind her and lightning lit up every corner of their beige-tone open-plan office. "But wow! Stay," she commanded, pointing to where Roland stood and running to the bathroom.

"Here," Jenn said, extending a large striped towel toward Roland, who grabbed a corner then wrapped his dripping head.

"Where is everybody?" he asked, "I mean, besides you and me."

Jenn smiled. She had to admit to herself that Roland was getting a little better about the way he communicated in the office—fewer general remarks that were really meant for one (usually Bill), fewer requests that began "when you get a minute . . ." or her favorite, "remind me to . . ." Because she hadn't figured out a way to remind Roland of anything. He seemed opposed to email, didn't text; pinging, forget it. Just that little notebook, that's all this former cop had. And now, she was sure, that was one blurry mess.

"Hard to know where anyone is . . . " Jenn said. "Whiteboards are useless if nobody fills them in. What did you guys do as cops?"

"Whiteboards." Roland deadpanned. "I know there's sharing software out there just for us—I just—"

"Yes, there is, I'm so glad you said that," Jenn interrupted. (How long had she been waiting for him to say something like this?) "Let me look into it."

Roland eased his wet jacket onto a hanger and took a thick sheaf of the Sunday classified section of the *Washington Post* from Bill's desk and pieced it carefully over his own chair seat.

"Why don't we have just a digital subscription?" Jenn asked. "No, wait. I get it," she said as she watched him arrange himself and settle into his chair.

"Good, saves my having to explain Gen Y and Baby Boomer differences," said Roland, taking off his glasses and drying them on a dry corner of shirttail.

Roland and Bill were still talking about how to expand the company to handle the sheer number of requests that were rolling into the agency. But now, besides the additional staff, any expansion would have to include the significant investments both in software and training that Jenn had recommended. Overwhelmed but happy, they enjoyed unending days divided between their office and case visits; it seemed they were working harder than they had on the police force. One late Friday night, both Roland and Bill were cleaning up a couple of client reports when Roland looked at his partner and said, "What's wrong with this picture?"

The following Tuesday, Dana sat in their offices as they spoke about working too hard. "Reminds me of the *E-Myth* story," Dana said.

"The what?" Bill replied.

She explained that in Michael Gerber's book *The E-Myth* there was a story about a woman who loved to bake pies. So, she opened up her own pie shop. She baked wonderful pies early in the morning and sold them the rest of the day. The more and better she got at making pies, the more she sold and the later she worked—it became a kind of vicious cycle. Soon she became a prisoner of her own creation and success. She'd created a business that required her physical presence all day, every day, instead of building a business that could operate without her.

"That story fits us to a T!" said Roland.

That's when Dana announced to Roland and Bill: "Look, I'm going to be the professor now—this is *not* coaching but teaching. You all good with that?"

The two gave her an "of course" nod.

Dana stood up next to the whiteboard in the conference room. She grabbed a black marker and drew and labeled two figures. The first she labeled the Motivation Pyramid and split it into three horizontal sections; the second figure she called the Motivation Matrix.

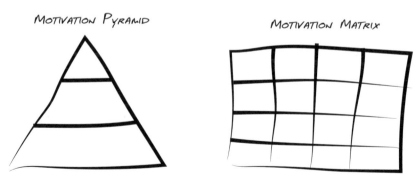

MOTIVATION PYRAMID                    MOTIVATION MATRIX

Dana then explained how Roland and Bill could grow but not be eaten alive by their own success. Now that they were at what she called "the teachable moment."

She explained that people have to feel satisfied first and foremost. Next people want to belong. "We're pack animals," she said. "Once satisfaction and social needs are established, then folks get confident, stimulated, experimental, and self-motivated. And that's where creativity is born. The big creative ideas only come when people are satisfied, social, and purpose driven," she said while underscoring each word in the pyramid.

Dana paused for a couple of seconds and looked at the duo, who both nodded that they were getting it. She explained that in a work environment the hierarchy for individuals was the same with some slight modification: people at work had to have their needs satisfied, had to be socially connected, and have purposeful work.

"I think we have all that here," Roland said brushing back his silver hair.

Bill agreed. "We all seem to get along and thrive on the casework."

Dana noted that she thought their assessment was correct to a point. "The problem you're running into is that you both are required for the magic to happen; for cases to come in the front door and go out the back door—solved."

The two owners looked at Dana as if to say, *So, OK, show us what we need to do already.*

Dana read their faces, nodded, and pointed to the third column on the Motivation Matrix, which she labeled "Teams."

"Right here is where you can shift the focus from individuals—namely you two superstars—to the team."

She explained that unless Roland and Bill could make this step, they'd end up like the pie lady in *The E-Myth*.

"To do that you have to fully support the team—give them the tools and tech support they need to make the company run. That means training your replacements!"

"Already putting us out to pasture!" Roland said.

"Nope, putting you out to get more work, hire more people, and expand the operation. That *is* what you said you wanted to do, right?"

Roland and Bill sheepishly nodded their heads.

Dana stopped there to give a bit of a sermonette. She told them about a man she'd worked with once who'd told Dana the same thing—he wanted to be less in the weeds of the operation. But when it really came time to hand over the reins, he had "founder's disease." Could not stop meddling in the very thing he'd created. Meddled so much that people quit, and eventually he closed down the business.

"So, if you guys are serious, I'll go on. Otherwise, let's get lunch and call it a day."

Bill spoke first, "Please, go on, we're serious." Roland nodded.

Dana explained that once fully supported, teams sought to be socially and collaboratively bonded. This is more than just connected—bonded means that they've become a single, collaborative, interdependent, and operating unit—all for one and one for all. The bond at this level gets intense and a clear team leader will emerge—not often the most vocal, but the most trusted.

Roland and Bill looked from each other to their coach, a look that meant there was no such person at Epps Security, yet.

Dana explained that fully supported and socially bonded, collaborative teams took on mission-centric problems. Such focused, mission-centric projects—like a tough case—bonded the team even further.

"When team members focus on something bigger than themselves, they grow into something bigger than themselves—it's that simple. They start molding the enduring culture of the business that the founders started into something bigger and better. And when that starts, the organization is prepared to grow into a self-sustaining organism—the innovative organization—one that can adapt to change and survive."

"So the more independent and bonded teams get, the more adaptive and innovative the business," Bill said.

"Up to a point," said Dana.

She went on to explain that if a company has a hub-and-spoke method of growth, it will never thrive. That is, if the founders stay at the center, nothing much changes, even if the teams get very focused. Often teams get strong but never connected—they become unconnected silos. That kind of organization kills the innovative process—blocking progress from creativity to fully functional innovation. That's why the fourth column in the matrix focuses on the organization.

"The innovative company is a special organism—one capable of adapting and sustaining itself," she said.

Dana explained that at its base such an innovative organization had to be organizationally stable—that is, there has to be stable leadership, structure, and processes. Additionally, there must be sufficient financial backing that allows the owners to expand, experiment, and even exit.

"Exit?" said Bill.

"Yes, eventually everyone has to say good-bye to the day-to-day operations if they want the business to grow and flourish."

"But isn't that like quitting on the business?" Roland asked.

"No, it's like when your parents drop you off at college. They were always there to support you, but the days of waking you up in the morning for high school are over. You have to learn to fly on your own. Same thing with companies—if they want to adapt and prosper, they have to be able to operate without founders."

"Hmm," Roland said, "I'm not sure I'm ready for that yet."

"I understand," said Dana, "but someday, sooner than you think, you'll have to make a decision: Do you want the company to grow up or do you want to keep it going as a lifestyle business—or just a well-paying hobby."

"Ouch," said Roland.

"My job is to tell you the truth, as I know it, not make you feel great."

"You're doing a great job of that then!" Roland said with a forced laugh.

Dana explained that in the innovative organization all the various teams had to be united—they needed to be culturally integrated. No matter what their individual team subculture was—their ways of operating, their symbols, their behaviors, traditions—they had to be united by an overarching set of rules and norms.

"Take the Methodist Church, the Girl Scouts, or Starbucks. There may be thousands of Methodist congregations, Girl Scout troops, or Starbucks teams around the country, but wherever you go they all have a particular way of operating—the way they do business that makes them uniquely part of the larger organization."

"OK, I think I get what you're saying," said Roland.

Dana explained that when you walk into a Starbucks in Idaho, it might have a particular set of pictures on the wall, the folks may have an accent, and it might even have some specialties and a "personality" all its own. However, when you order a grande Pike Place Roast, you want it to taste like the one you had in Seattle or in Boston.

"But it's bigger than that," she said. "Starbucks has a particular language, a dress code of sorts, the way you line up, a kind of an attitude of hipness, all add to the culture that makes it different from McDonald's. You guys will want all your culturally integrated teams to have a single vision to focus on."

"That vision can be established by the founders," she explained, "but it's better evolved by the market and the organization's teams as they see the opportunity to adapt and adjust their vision to meet a changing environment."

"So, at one point," Dana said, "Starbucks might have wanted to make the most robust coffee on the planet. But now it might want to be America's brand of coffee—something like that."

"Vision comes best when you ask, 'what do we want to become?' It should unify the various team missions into a single, aspirational vision of the future," she said.

"I'm getting a headache," said Bill, to which both Roland and Dana laughed.

"Fair enough," Dana said, "enough strategy for today. Just remember the pie lady in *The E-Myth*!"

Both men smiled and nodded.

"So, what's your mission, guys?" asked Dana.

"Catch bad guys doing bad things," Roland said without much of a thought.

Dana looked at Bill.

"I guess that's it."

"Not sure that would inspire me to follow you guys off a cliff or to dive from a burning bridge," Dana replied. "Let's try it again. What's your noble purpose?"

"Huh?" Bill asked.

"Why do you guys exist?"

"To catch bad guys!" Roland insisted.

"Wrong, that's a result, not a purpose. Not the 'why' you do it."

"We do it because people deserve a big brother in their corner to protect them from bullies and bad guys. That's why I do it," Bill said.

"Much better!" said Dana.

"I do it because I don't like people who prey on weaker ones. Kind of what Bill just said," Roland piped in.

"So, the agency's purpose is to protect and defend clients less able to take care of themselves. Is that in the ballpark?"

"Yep, 'protect and defend' used to be on our squad cars in the police department," Roland said.

"That's your noble cause. People will follow that lead more than just 'catch bad guys.' Protect and defend is a purpose that gives a team and an organization something to aspire to—a higher calling or a noble purpose."

Over the next few weeks, Roland and Bill spent a lot of time thinking about what Dana had asked them—why they exist; their real purpose. The two had thought about their purpose long and hard and came up with something they thought was elegant and memorable: We exist to serve, protect, and offer citizens a private security option to solve their most difficult professional and personal security problems.

Working with Dana at now more than a half dozen off-sites, the company finally settled on their collective vision:

WE ARE THE PRIVATE DETECTIVE AGENCY OF CHOICE IN NORTHERN VIRGINIA BECAUSE WE SERVE AND PROTECT ITS CITIZENS BY OFFERING THEM A PRIVATE SECURITY OPTION TO SOLVE THEIR MOST DIFFICULT PROFESSIONAL AND PERSONAL PROBLEMS.

The team's purpose, vision, and values made it not only distinctive but also attractive to a wide clientele. But their success with a particularly delicate case elevated the agency in a way the partners couldn't have planned.

A foreign diplomat thought that his wife was being unfaithful with a local, popular florist. Through surveillance the team was able to prove to him that she was actually planning an elaborate 50th birthday for him—her overly jealous husband. Following the very discreet investigation, the wealthy diplomat offered the PI firm a seven-figure, no-interest credit loan, a common cultural practice with family and close friends. After some organizational advice from Dana and due diligence from their attorney, the partners graciously accepted the loan and ramped up their agency from a handful to 10 people, including contract investigators. They now had the ability to step away from the day-to-day operations, just as Dana had advised them, and avoid pie-lady syndrome.

## THE STORY: The Case of the AWOL Inventory

Roland and Bill were settling into their respective roles. Bill was taking care of business—paying bills, hiring, and handling all the administrative duties of a PI agency. Roland was Mr. Business Development—getting new business clients and going undercover anytime possible. Regularly attending networking and committee meetings at the local chamber of commerce, Roland soon found himself on their board of directors.

The cases seemed almost to float into Roland's hands. Recently, he got a call from a trucking company owned by one of his old criminal informants, Lou Spagnolla, who'd been grooming his eldest son, Alfie (Alfonso), to take over the business for as many years as Roland could remember. And Alfie kidded that he'd been groomed to death! The company mostly shipped auto parts from dealerships to third-party repair garages around Northern Virginia. So, when Joe's Auto Shop wanted original Honda brakes or mufflers, Lou's company bought and delivered them, after adding a markup.

It seemed like the perfect business for Lou after his prison stint. He'd been sentenced quickly after turning state's evidence in a car-theft ring case that Roland had broken, and, as Bill often pointed out, Roland had a soft spot for ex-cons like Lou, for whom most things in life were hard. But he'd been a model citizen these 20 years.

Twenty years. Bill had been brought in to work that car-theft case, with Roland under cover, and the two became partners afterward. Roland thought there wasn't any cop more solid, by the book, and reliable than his new partner, Bill, who, on the other hand, found Roland pretty much the opposite: flamboyant, chatty, and too good looking.

When Bill complained to Sandra, his wife, she confirmed the worst: "But you two *are* opposites," she said, rushing to add, "in a good way." It wasn't too long before Bill agreed.

And over time ex-con Lou Spagnolla became a touchstone for the partners by which they viewed time passing, for themselves and their careers.

When Lou called Roland this time, he confided that he'd noticed inventory seemed to be running short. A piece missing here and there, but still the books added up. So he started to investigate on his own and found that for the previous three months the company had delivered 52 Toyota brake pads, but only 48 could be accounted for. After finding a three-month trend of past shortages, Lou thought it was time to contact his old friend Roland.

Roland took the initial complaint and then asked Lou to hire a "new" guy—in reality, the agency's forensic accountant specialist, Dan, undercover. Dan had a Harley and his share of tattoos—full sleeves and some cool ink on his neck and chest. He may have been trained in accounting, but he looked like he should be in the wrestling ring. Dan's undercover backstory was that he'd done some time in prison for stolen cars—and he looked every bit the part. Everyone at the company knew that Lou favored ex-cons, so Dan's story floated well.

But when Alfie got back in town from a short vacation and learned of the thefts, he went ballistic.

"Damn it, Dad, I had Tony all ready to take care of the inventory. One glitch and you hire a new guy. You have the patience of a gnat!"

"You watch your mouth with me!"

"Dad, I'll handle it. Where's the new guy?"

"He's helping me with the books, accounts receivable, and inventory."

"I'm in charge of inventory!"

"And I own the company . . . I want another look at things."

"So, you don't trust me!"

"I'm just trying to figure out what's going on."

Alfie threw down the pen in his hand and stormed out of the office.

A week went by with Dan settling in, and Alfie avoiding both his father and Dan. However, surprisingly, the following Friday the inventory showed no shortage at all.

Lou called his son into his office, where Roland was sitting, along with Dan.

Without a word of greeting, Alfie arrived and looked from one man to the other, as if they were intruders.

"What's going on, Dad? What's the newbie doing here, and who's the suit?" he said looking at Roland, who nodded.

"Sit down, Alfonso," Lou said without allowing much room for debate. Alfie sat.

"Watch this," Lou said, nodding to Dan, who hit the mouse on the computer and ran the video. The time and date stamp showed 2 a.m. on Monday—the day after the follow-up inventory by Dan. Alfie could be clearly seen parking his personal car, unlocking the door to the warehouse, and loading brake pads into the trunk.

"What's going on, son?"

"I . . . was . . . just going to rearrange the stock on Tuesday, is all."

"Bull!" Lou said.

"Dad, I was just . . ."

"Do NOT lie to me."

"OK . . . all right! I needed some extra money to cover a bet with my bookie. I was going to repay. Honest."

"Stop, no more lies. If you weren't my kid, I'd . . . "

"Ahem," Roland interrupted.

"I'm just saying . . ." Lou said, "I can't believe you'd steal from your own family. I would have covered your bets if you'd just asked me."

"But Dad, you pay me crap, and . . ."

"Just get out, NOW. I'll deal with you later."

After Alfie left, Roland said, "Lou, I'm so sorry. I was hoping this would end differently."

"Do you know what Alfonso means in Italian?" Lou asked of no one in particular. "Noble and ready! I guess not! Look, thanks for your good work, especially Dan, thank you."

Dan nodded, then headed for his Harley parked in the lot.

Roland lingered in the doorway. "I don't want to tell you how to run your business, Lou, I know it's rough."

"You have no idea," Lou said, exhaling deeply then stopped, "No, I guess you do." He had always been a big guy, and Roland was sure he could bench press more than any of the guys in the warehouse, but right now he looked fragile and helpless.

"Just call this person," Roland said as he reached in his wallet and withdrew a crisp umber-colored business card.

"Executive coach, huh?" Lou peered at the card he held in both hands.

"Why not? Worth a shot, right?" Roland said, trying to sound casual, and not veer any closer to the heart of Lou's business, and his business problem, than he already had.

"What you always say," said Lou.

Driving off, Roland shook his head and muttered, "Why not, worth a shot." The fact was Roland could bet that Dana, who said business is about asking the right questions, would have a whole set of them for Lou.

**Roland's Notes**

- [ ] DETERMINE WHAT'S IN THEIR HEART—THE CORE OF THEIR PURPOSE.
- [ ] "LITTLE BETS" CAN LEAD TO BIG IDEAS.
- [ ] CULTURE BOILS DOWN TO ARTIFACTS, ESPOUSED BELIEFS, AND BASIC ASSUMPTIONS.
- [ ] REMOVE BARRIERS AND PROVIDE SUPPORT.
- [ ] WHAT IS YOUR NOBLE PURPOSE?
- [ ] NO MONEY, NO MISSION. NO INNOVATION, NO FUTURE COMPANY.

| Roland's Notes (continued) |
| --- |

☐ Vision comes best when you ask, "What do we want to become?"

☐ But a vision without a plan for execution is a form of delusion.

☐ Avoid becoming the pie lady.

☐ Did Lou have founder's disease?

# References

Amabile, T.M., and S.J. Kramer. 2011. *The Progress Principle: Using Small Wins to Ignite Joy, Engagement, and Creativity at Work*. Boston: Harvard Business Review Press.

Berg, J.M., J.E. Dutton, and A. Wrzesniewski. 2007. "What Is Job Crafting and Why Does It Matter?" Regents of the University of Michigan. http://positiveorgs.bus.umich.edu/wp-content/uploads/What-is-Job-Crafting-and-Why-Does-it-Matter1.pdf.

Cameron, K.S., and R.E. Quinn. 2011. *Diagnosing and Changing Organizational Culture: Based on the Competing Values Framework*. 3rd ed. San Francisco: Jossey-Bass.

Cashman, K. 2008. *Leadership From the Inside Out: Becoming a Leader for Life*. 2nd ed. San Francisco: Berrett-Koehler.

Catmull, E. 2014. *Creativity, Inc.: Overcoming the Unseen Forces That Stand in the Way of True Inspiration*. New York: Random House.

Cialdini, R.B. 2006. *Influence: The Psychology of Persuasion*. Rev. ed. Boston: Harper Business.

Covey, S.R. 2013. *The 7 Habits of Highly Effective People: Powerful Lessons in Personal Change* (25th Anniversary Edition). New York: RosettaBooks.

Fernández-Aráoz, C. 2014. *It's Not the How or the What but the Who: Succeed by Surrounding Yourself With the Best*. Boston: Harvard Business Review Press.

Gerber, M.E. 2009. *The E-Myth Revisited: Why Most Small Businesses Don't Work and What to Do About It*. New York: HarperCollins e-books.

Govindarajan, V., and C. Trimble. 2010. *The Other Side of Innovation: Solving the Execution Challenge*. Boston: Harvard Business Review Press.

Herzberg, F. 1987. "One More Time: How Do You Motivate Employees?" *Harvard Business Review*, September–October. Reprint Number 87507.

Hill, L.A., G. Brandeau, E. Truelove, and K. Lineback. 2014. *Collective Genius: The Art and Practice of Leading Innovation*. Boston: Harvard Business Review Press.

Kouzes, J.M., and B.Z. Posner. 2012. *The Leadership Challenge: How to Make Extraordinary Things Happen in Organizations*. 5th ed. San Francisco: Jossey-Bass.

Lieberman, M.D. 2013. *Social: Why Our Brains Are Wired to Connec*t. New York: Crown.

Lyubomirsky, S. 2007. *The How of Happiness: A New Approach to Getting the Life You Want*. New York: Penguin.

Maslow, A.H. 2011. *Hierarchy of Needs: A Theory of Human Motivation*.

Pentland, A. 2014. *Social Physics: How Good Ideas Spread—The Lessons From a New Science*. New York: Penguin.

Rowley, T. 2014. "A Bridge Half-Way Across a River Is a Diving Board!" Vice president, Cardinal Bank in board meeting at Fairfax County, VA, Chamber of Commerce, February 12.

Sawyer, K. 2007. *Group Genius: The Creative Power of Collaboration*. New York: Basic Books.

Schein, E.H. 2010. *Organizational Culture and Leadership*. 4th ed. San Francisco: Jossey-Bass.

Sims, P. 2011. *Little Bets: How Breakthrough Ideas Emerge From Small Discoveries*. New York: Simon & Schuster.

# 4

# THE INNOVATION EQUATION
# PART 3: THE PROCESS

Creative talent working in a motivating environment is not sufficient to generate sustainable, value-based innovation. There is a third factor that needs to be involved in the equation: Having a reliable, repeatable development process that creates value from the initial idea. For many years, executive coaches have helped leaders and teams solve all manner of problems, make changes, and innovate by asking critical questions, not by giving advice, which is what consultants do. To develop a reliable, repeatable development process, three proven models, each supported by research, can be integrated to form an innovation hybrid. The three models are the coach-approach model, action learning, and entrepreneurship.

## The Coach-Approach Model

Whether you're talking about design thinking, business problem solving, or coaching, the landscape is populated by models, too numerous to reference here, to help people and teams solve problems. To get a handle on just how many models are out there, Google "problem-solving model," "design thinking," and "coaching model." Next click "images" and watch the hundreds of models that appear. It's staggering! And while some writers may think they have invented a particular model, models stand on the shoulders of many people. After reviewing many such models, I constructed one that I call the coach approach (Gladis 2012), which has been taught to many leaders and teams, with proven success. Simply put, this model focuses on asking questions that elicit conversation and discussion—the lifeblood of coaching. Such questions as who, what, and how—open-ended questions—help clients talk through their problems. The model also segments the process into four parts: issue (defining the problem or issue); impact of the present state; ideal possible future state; and finally, intention or plan going forward. Again, it's a derivative model that emerged from studying many coaching and problem-solving models. Its similarity to many other models and its efficacy give it validity and reliability.

## Action Learning

The power of questions has solved the world's great problems. For example, the legendary Cavendish Physics Labs at the University of Cambridge, which over the years has produced an astonishing 29 Nobel laureates—innovators of the highest order—employs a group question-asking method called "action learning." It was developed in the 1940s by physicist turned management thinker Reg Revans, who wanted to understand how such vaunted scientists treated each other in the labs. Turns out that instead of being boastful, know-it-all bores, they were respectful and asked lots of questions. Revans later applied the action learning technique to his work with the National Coal Board, where he encouraged the use of best practices. According to Revans' Law, for an organization to survive, its rate of learning must be equal to the rate of change in its surrounding environment. A latter-day Revans devotee, Michael Marquardt is an action learning guru and professor at George Washington University. He leads a group called the World Institute for Action Learning, aimed at spreading the word and teaching the technique to teachers, trainers, and leaders.

## Entrepreneurship

For years there have often been two folks in a garage inventing the next big thing. Most times, their great idea runs out of steam and money—

usually about the same time. Back in the dot-com crazy gold-rush days, things took a different turn. Everyone wanted to get into the get-rich-quick world of dot-com startups. Accordingly, venture capitalists and private equity investors caught the fever of this new economy and due to some early money makers, invested in young bright kids with big ideas and tossed a lot of money at their early-stage ideas. Then these entrepreneurs went into seclusion and developed new models, businesses, and programs intended to change the world overnight. One day when they launched their fully developed idea on the world, something strange happened—it flopped! Nobody bought it, and it didn't take long for venture capital money to start drying up. Welcome to the dot-com bubble burst of 1999-2001—a modern-day lesson in how the "fool's gold" of the Gold Rush days in 1849 could be repeated 150 years later—all because of greed and poor process.

Enter Steve Blank, who had been working for many years in Silicon Valley. A serial entrepreneur, Blank has ridden the tech business through the dot-com era and then some. He's started eight companies and has taken four of them public. He's since become wealthy and teaches at Stanford University—two states of being not usually found in the same person—and is considered the father of the customer development model and the lean start-up movement, which was coined by one of his students and collaborators, Eric Ries. The lean start-up approach uses such steps as developing a minimum viable product (MVP); experimentation, measurement, and iteration; early customer exposure and feedback; and more. Anyone interested in taking a free lean start-up course by Blank can do so by visiting his website or going to "How to Build a Startup" on Udacity (www.udacity.com/courses/all).

In the next chapter, the innovation discussion about process heats up with the introduction of the 5Ps Innovation Development Process—derived from these very coaching, problem-solving, and entrepreneurial processes.

As for the PI team at Epps Security, they've tried their hand at action learning, they've refined their business plan, and tried to align it with the vision statement they'd crafted with Dana's help. So why are they still having problems?

## THE STORY: Sowing Seeds but Growing Pains, or Questions, Questions, Questions

The season was fall, but as she maneuvered her car into the shade Dana noticed that the trees bordering the parking lot had undergone no observable change. The afternoon air was as heavy as August, and the street quiet. School had been back in session for more than a month; summer vacation a distant memory.

Dana didn't have to look at her watch to know that Roland was late. They'd agreed to meet for coffee because he had questions for her, he said, that he couldn't ask on the phone. Here's how that phone call went:

"Office is getting too noisy, can't hear myself think," he said.

"The sound of progress! You sound old and crotchety," she said, teasing.

"How'd you know I have a birthday coming?"

"Hah! Maybe it's time you guys invested in some wall units; all that open space could be bad for your health. Business health, I mean."

But just as she mused about their latest call, Roland whisked in. "Sorry to be late," he said, leaning over her, his hand lightly tapped her shoulder. "What I get for having questions."

"What kind of questions?" Dana pushed her chair back and faced him.

"How do I say no?"

"How do you what?"

"Say no to a client, to a case, when I've been a cop forever, and never, ever have walked away from a case that needs solving, or someone who needed help. Cops don't do that."

"But . . ."

"It's no good to say I'm not a cop, because——"

"——you'll always be a cop," Dana said and smiled, touching his hand. "I get it."

"So do I have a business problem or a psychological problem?"

"Wow. A good question," Dana paused and studied Roland. He was the only cop she knew. "What do you think?"

"Maybe I just like things the way they are," Roland said and shrugged.

"Hmm. It can be hard to be a focused leader," Dana said, sitting back but giving Roland her full attention. "Daniel Goleman writes a lot about the link between attention and excellence. He says that focused leaders have to control their own feelings and impulses, the way others see them, understand what others need from them, all the while getting rid of distractions—and any preconceptions that get in the way."

"I've got preconceptions?" Roland looked at her as if to say, really?

"Perhaps that you are only a cop," Dana said. "Your attention in this new enterprise, for example, requires for the first time different leadership skills . . . emotional, organizational, strategic . . . Just saying . . . first time anyone's asked you to do this."

"But it was my idea . . ."

"Which is why you should read Goleman."

<hr/>

At the team meeting, the question came from the front of the room. "What is the problem?" The voice speaking was Jenn's, musing and inquisitive as she read from the whiteboard. Her nose was inches from the board, and she could reach out and touch its shiny surface, even smudge out the words she didn't understand, least of all agree with.

> WE ARE THE PRIVATE DETECTIVE AGENCY OF CHOICE IN NORTHERN
> VIRGINIA BECAUSE WE SERVE AND PROTECT ITS CITIZENS BY OFFER—
> ING THEM AN EXCELLENT PRIVATE SECURITY OPTION TO SOLVE THEIR
> MOST DIFFICULT PROFESSIONAL AND PERSONAL PROBLEMS.

"It's a noble goal," Jenn said, then turned around to face her colleagues. "But it's not all we do."

Besides Roland, Bill, and Dan, there was now Ryan, an investigator going to law school at night, and Jenn's friend Rachel, who was doing medical case background research most days.

To stay sharp and focused, Dana had suggested weekly meetings around the whiteboard as the group further refined its purpose.

"So, is that the problem?" Dan asked. "Or can we just rewrite that statement?"

"Just rewrite you say? Spoken like an accountant," said Ryan, looking up from his laptop. "No offense, and I understand the temptation to change as the business grows and evolves, but mission is attached to foundation. So, add to it, if you like, but don't redo it. My opinion."

"Roland and Bill," Jenn addressed the founding partners, "you two more than the rest of us created that statement. The thing is, it's not . . . or let me rephrase . . . is it who you are?"

Bill and Roland looked at each other and scratched their heads almost in unison.

Just then the office phone rang. Roland leaned over to answer it just as the *Dragnet* ringtone on his own smartphone went off.

"Jack! Jack Henderson! Of course, sure I do." At the mention of this name from their collective past, Bill jolted to attention.

"I'm sorry, no, I didn't know," Roland continued. "Sure, sure . . . yes, he does . . . we can . . . sounds good, see you then."

Roland turned to Bill. "He'd like us both to come by this afternoon. Same office down on University near Town Hall. But Dan, you should come too, sounds like up your alley."

Dan nodded and stood up as if ready to go. "Gotta be fraud."

"It is," said Roland, "and he won't go to the cops."

"You know why," said Bill. "Our favorite chief."

"So our whiteboard meeting's adjourned for now," said Jenn matter-of-factly. "That's cool. There are some background checks that need to go out today."

"And I'm still on surveillance detail with Spagnolla Auto Parts," said Ryan. At Lou's request, an investigator had taken over for Dan and gone undercover in the warehouse to continue the investigation. Lou had a hunch that his son wasn't acting alone.

"How's that going anyway?" Bill asked. "Do you really think Lou's right—that others in the warehouse are involved?"

"Alfie has a lot of friends there, and you might say that employee morale isn't great," said Ryan. "Lots of micromanaging if you ask me, not much trust."

"Sounds like a job for one Dana Glass!" exclaimed Dan. And Roland smiled.

"You guys," said Roland. "I mean Ryan, Jenn, and Rachel," he paused, looking over at his partner for affirmation. "We appreciate your input. So, what would you add to the mission statement? Think about answering that question."

"A can of worms," Bill muttered as the two detectives walked to the car that afternoon. "That's what you opened up back there."

"No, we have to try this," Roland said easily, as if he half expected Bill's response. "You'll see. They want to help us—we have to let them," he said. "They'll add—they won't subtract."

"How can you be so sure?" Bill asked.

"Good question," Roland said, stopping to face his partner. "I'm sure because we have the same goal. To create a reliable and repeatable process," he said, pointing to his head.

Later that afternoon, as Roland drove down Lee Highway toward Jack Henderson's office, he and Bill filled in Dan on the local real estate agent and the missing person case of his first wife.

"I remember my parents talking about that case. Just because it was high society and odd," said Dan. "So is she still showing dogs?"

"Now you're making me feel old," said Roland. "The first wife mostly breeds dogs now, less in the ring. She sends me pictures of pups she's training from time to time. I was close to getting one once, but I was traveling a lot and changed my mind."

"Not so much now," said Bill. "You could make room in your life for a furry friend."

"You think? How about you and Sandra?" asked Roland.

"I think she'd rather travel than get a dog," said Bill.

"You guys," interrupted Dan, "don't forget to bring me up to speed on our case."

"Our case," began Roland. "Jack Henderson, happily married to Maddie these 10 years, has been estranged from his father because of said marriage. Jack's father, who had moved to Florida, died there rather suddenly last month."

"How old?" asked Dan.

"Father? Maybe 75. The issue, and this is where you come in, Dan, is the deceased's accounts. Jack is John Stewart Henderson III, and as we all know, banks and probate sometimes can get confused by too many people having the same name," said Roland.

"Even when their ages are different, or their socials," said Bill shaking his head.

"But sometimes not," said Dan. "Is that what you're saying? Someone's gotten in touch with Jack about his accounts, pretending to be from the father's bank?"

"Bingo," said Roland. "But he might be from the bank legitimately, and might be making a good faith attempt to try to figure out what's going on."

"This is where I come in," said Dan. "Figure out who's who, why, and how much. Cool."

"The only thing is," said Roland, "When you pretend to be Jack, you've got to hide the fact that he's been disinherited."

---

Jack Henderson was tall and fit and the small boy wrapped around his ankles when he answered the detectives' knock at the door had the same unruly blond hair.

"Come in, come in," Jack said hoisting the child on his hip and extending a hand toward Roland first and then Bill. "Thanks for coming by on such short notice."

"Jack, this is Dan Cullen," said Roland. "He's a forensic accountant and can help with your father's case."

"Can he have a case if a person's dead?" asked Jack. "No disrespect, dad and I hadn't seen eye to eye over the last several years, but he still had business interests, employees relying on him, and he's not the kind of guy who would take advantage of them."

"Have you received any phone calls or just emails?" asked Bill.

"Just official-looking emails from a bank claiming to be his," said Jack. "I'll show you everything on my laptop, but this bank account manager claims that my father's account has been suddenly drained by close to a million dollars, company assets just disappeared."

"Show me," said Dan. While Roland and Bill asked Jack more questions and took notes, Dan scrutinized the emails that Jack had received. "So you asked for the financial statements and they attached a few," Dan said. "What about the business accounts?"

"There are a couple partners," said Jack, "but I've not been able to reach them."

"Well, that seems kind of obvious, don't you think?" asked Dan, and Roland shot him a quizzical look.

"No," said Jack. "They're family—my uncles. His brothers. There's been no falling out there, if that's what you mean."

"But you didn't hear from them when your father died? Doesn't that seem kind of strange?" asked Dan. Once again, a questioning look from Roland.

"No, because they're not well men," said Jack patiently. "They're both in a nursing home in Florida, which is why my father moved there, to be closer to them, but for all intents and purposes, they're more silent partners."

"How old are they?"

"Should be 83 and 86 this year," said Jack.

"So, . . . no disrespect," said Dan, carefully closing the laptop lid. "But it's possible that everyone's a silent partner, wouldn't you say?"

Roland again looked askance at his young associate. "What Dan is suggesting," Roland said in his best surmising tone, turning to face Jack, "is that your uncles, as well as your father, could all be . . . ummm . . . deceased."

"It's just a hunch . . . I'm so sorry," said Dan. "Cases like this . . .

I mean, I have a hunch that something was perp . . . that something occurred." He stood there suddenly reluctant to say more.

"In the nursing home?" asked Bill.

"Yes, that's what I think," said Dan.

"So Dan will be on the next plane down there," said Roland. "We're so sorry, but together we'll solve this."

"Well, thanks," said Jack. "For all your help. I've always felt that I could count on you." He stopped, shaking his head. "And you know, I must have felt that I could count on them, too, that we had time to resolve our differences. To have them all gone, at once, it's a very empty feeling. I'm not proud to say that I left things undone."

The four men then walked gingerly, heads down, to the front door, especially careful to avoid the small blond boy scurrying on all fours in front of them.

Roland and Bill were impressed with how swiftly Dan had been able to close the case. The young accountant's hunch from that initial visit was on the mark: The brothers Henderson had died within a week of each other; Jack's father first, from an inherited physical condition he had managed to keep secret for years, and then his uncles coincidentally from natural causes in the nursing home, where the account fraud was quickly perpetrated by a once-loyal assistant who'd fallen behind on her scheduled college-loan repayments. Having a bit of college debt himself, Dan was haunted by the young woman's story. He shared his findings with the Florida bank account manager, who was able to confirm dates and withdrawals. But the best news, Dan reported on his return, was that there would be an heir to the found Henderson fortune after all, Jack's young son.

**Roland's Notes**

☐ Third factor in the Innovation Equation is a reliable, repeatable process.

☐ To survive, an organization's rate of learning must be equal to the rate of change in its surrounding environment.

☐ Open-ended questions help clients talk through their problems.

☐ The power of questions has solved the world's great problems.

☐ Create value and repeat.

# References

Blank, S. 2013. *The Four Steps to the Epiphany: Successful Strategies for Products That Win.* 2nd ed. Pescadero, CA: K&S Ranch.

———. 2010. *Not All Those Who Wander Are Lost: Posts From an Entrepreneurial Career.* https://steveblank.com/2010/02/18/not-all-those-who-wander-are-lost.

———, and B. Dorf. 2012. *The Startup Owner's Manual: The Step-by-Step Guide for Building a Great Company.* Pescadero, CA: K&S Ranch.

Marquardt, M.J. 2014. *Leading With Questions: How Leaders Find the Right Solutions by Knowing What to Ask.* San Francisco: Jossey-Bass.

———. 2011. *Optimizing the Power of Action Learning: Real-Time Strategies for Developing Leaders, Building Teams and Transforming Organizations.* 2nd ed. Boston: Nicholas Brealey.

Revans, R. 2011. *ABC of Action Learning.* Burlington, VT: Gower.

# 5

# THE INNOVATION EQUATION PART 3: THE PROCESS CONTINUES

Think of how mountain bikes evolved. A group of kids from Northern California wanted to ride up and down hill trails, so they needed wide tires from their fathers' bikes to absorb the shock, combined with the gears of 10 speeds to climb the hills. That mashup became the mountain bike, which is now a nearly $60 billion business. In somewhat similar fashion, the model presented here—the 5Ps Innovation Development Process—was derived from a mashup of well-developed coaching, problem-solving, and entrepreneurial models.

So to recap the **Innovation Equation: I = T + E + P**. You take a promising idea, gather Talented people, who are cognitively diverse, engaged, and have a growth mindset. Put them in an Environment that is safe, supportive, and purposeful. Then finally, give them an effective and efficient Process—capable of replication that is reliable. Here's what the process looks like, once you've taken care of talent and the environment.

## The 5Ps Innovation Development Process

The 5Ps Innovation Development Process consists of asking questions—not giving answers. Such a question-based process elicits thinking, reflection, discussion, experimentation, and reiteration. Questions like who, what, how, and open-ended questions—not answers or judgments—

get to innovation much faster because they open up the options (divergent thinking) instead of narrowing thinking too quickly (convergent thinking).

Like executive coaches, innovative leaders need a process or framework to help their teams through a problem-solving cycle that can produce change—without producing anxiety and resistance, which shuts down creativity. Using the leader as the coach, who ensures that people ask questions and does not offer advice, the process involves five steps: problem, present, possible, plan, and pivot (Figure 5-1).

Figure 5-1: The 5Ps Innovation Development Process

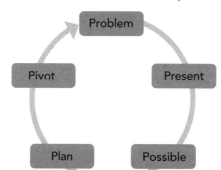

## Problem or Opportunity

The leader-coach needs to ensure that the first round of questions in this process works toward getting a precise description of the problem or opportunity that has emerged. Note that the best opportunities usually start out as perceived problems. Consider the lightbulb, the automobile, and the computer. Each evolved to solve a problem: the need to have light at night, to have a mode of effective transportation, and to process massive amounts of data quickly. Maybe it's a problem begging for a new phone app, a product to reduce labor costs, or a technique to teach kids math. Identifying the problem—the real problem—is critical. As Harvard professor and leadership and innovation guru Clayton Christensen might say: What's the real job I would "hire" this product or service to do? Most often, people on the team have very different views of what the real problem is. With a good leader-coach, teams are pushed to ask thoughtful questions that can help define, clarify, and agree on the problem before trying to solve it. The problem presenter (discussed later in the appendix) and the group have to agree on what question they will tackle. Be sure to invest ample time on this step or suffer the consequences of wasted time and effort. An elegant solution to the wrong problem is simply a distraction.

## Present State

Next, describing the present state of the problem or opportunity provides a baseline, a kind of place from which to launch. Teams have to inventory the present state with a clear eye on what's already been done. With doctoral students, it's called doing a literature search or finding out who's already researched your topic of interest before launching a huge product only to discover the same thing already exists. In short, avoid trying to reinvent the wheel. Ask questions: What's the present state of the problem? Who's involved? How much does it cost? What's been done so far? What other companies have tackled this problem? What's the cost of doing nothing? On a scale from 1 to 10, how big a problem is this? Again, teams need to conduct an inventory of the present state of the problem or opportunity before moving to the next step—the possible future. The leader-coach needs to insist on the team asking a lot of questions like a reporter or a detective to uncover a clear picture of the present state.

## Possible Future

Often teams can get stuck in the present state of the current problem. Bogged down might better describe teams that get mired in the details of the problem. One job of the leader-coach is to push the team toward what might be, or could be, toward what's possible in the future. Pushing through this part of the innovative process is easier for some than others. Highly intuitive people enjoy this part of the process—they're swimming freely in their strengths when imagining possibilities. However, more practical, grounded people are less comfortable imagining what might be and sometimes feel like they're swimming in mud! Thus, leaders will have to push some people more than others. Here are some questions that help:

What's the possible future state look like? Who will be involved? What will be going on in the ideal possible future if we create and scale production of the best process or product? Staying open to all that's possible is difficult for some people, but the leader-coach must push the team to think wide and deep—to take off their blinders and imagine what's possible.

## Plan the Next Steps

Now the leader-coach needs to challenge the team to take action, if only to take some small first steps. Often grand, sweeping steps can intimidate people and create anxiety and resistance. So at the first meeting of the group, leaders need to have patience and ask people to take it one step at a time—an approach that's manageable.

It's important to note that the first iteration of this innovation development process is just that—a start—with more team gatherings to come. No strategy (or goals and objectives) comes right away; strategy only emerges over time with experimentation, learning, and recalibration. That's why taking a lot of time to craft a complex business plan in a room by yourself before ever talking to customers and experimenting is often a waste of time. Some people have difficulty with the word *experimentation*, but we do it all the time in our lives. We hear from the weatherperson that it's cold outside, so we experiment by wearing a particular coat. But when we get outside, we discover it feels a lot colder with the wind, so we go back in to get a heavier coat.

Ask some questions of the team: What's the plan going forward? What's one simple experiment or test we could run to test our hypothesis? Who on our team should do what next? When should we meet again? This planning step is all about creating momentum and accountability—just do it—do something. Who will do what, by when, and how will the team know it was done? These questions lead to advancing the innovation and accountability.

The coach then will ask each person what he or she will do before the next meeting. It's important that everyone be invested—that everyone takes actions that move the team toward a solution. In essence, the team owns the problem, and so all must work to solve it. Usually, people step up and offer to do some research, make some calls, interview or survey people in their own areas of responsibility, and report back at the next meeting. Thus, the leader-coach would do well to ask what specific clients might be useful to expose to the innovation and by when.

## Pivot or Adapt

This step includes all the activity and research team members do before the next meeting—to then meet and discuss what they discovered. *Pivoting* is a basketball term. Keeping one foot planted or rooted where you are, you turn or pivot in a new direction toward a potential opportunity. The term *pivot* was coined by Eric Ries as part of the experimental process he advocates for developing an MVP (minimum viable product—sort of like a rough draft) to show customers. After input from the customer, team members pivot and adapt to lessons learned from the customer—and report back at the next action team gathering. And, if the team expects redirection, they are less likely to become disappointed or frustrated too early in the process. Steve Blank calls the process of working with the customer right from the start "customer development." Just showing our ideas (MVP) to potential clients will modify plans right away, causing us to pivot in the direction of customer needs. As Blank says so often: "No business plan survives first contact with customers." Or as Mike Tyson says: "Everyone has a plan 'till they get punched in the mouth."

Because much of the 5Ps Innovation Development Process derives from action learning, individual development and learning cannot be forgotten in the midst of innovation. The individual participant learns much by simply participating in the inquiry and action to solve the problem. The group learns as it faces the problem, answers questions, and adds to its knowledge base. The organization learns as group members spread the learning-and-inquiry process throughout. Thus, learning is leveraged throughout the organization. Such innovative groups are safe places for leaders to practice.

What are the competencies learned in action learning and the 5Ps Innovation Development Process? Drawing from Michael Marquardt's seminal book, *Optimizing the Power of Action Learning: Real-Time Strategies for Developing Leaders, Building Teams and Transforming Organizations,* here is a summary of learning that happens in the process:

You can't change a system without changing yourself. Actions change the system and the actors. The key skills learned in the action learning innovative process are reflection, decision making, systems thinking, active listening, self-awareness, empathy, presentation, and facilitation, to mention only a few.

Much of what we acquire in the process of action learning aligns with the research and work of Daniel Goleman on emotional and social intelligence: self-awareness (self-observation and understanding one's own strengths and challenges), managing emotions (coping effectively with emotions such as fear, anxiety, anger, and sadness), motivating oneself (staying charged with enthusiasm), empathy (being sensitive to the feelings of others), and developing relationships (managing the emotions of others in the context of a relationship).

Teams learn shared commitments to solving problems, clarifying problems, willingness to work with others to solve problems and develop strategies, courage to ask the tough question, respect of others, willingness to learn and help others, and how to establish trust in the group.

Action learning helps build a learning organization. According to Marquardt, such a learning organization has four components:

1. **Increased learning skills**: Groups develop learning skills by learning! The process is recombinant much like DNA—learning creates better, faster learning.

2. **Transformed organizational culture and structure**: Action learning groups act independently and democratically with a minimum of structure and hierarchy. Along the journey, they create new culture and values (inquiry, experimentation, and so forth), which infects and affects the organization.

3. **Involvement of the entire business chain in the learning process**: Action learning can and does often involve customers,

suppliers, vendors, and others in the learning process. Opening up the boundaries makes possibilities much richer.

4. **Enhanced capability to manage knowledge:** Action learning helps members learn and practice how to acquire knowledge, create knowledge, store knowledge, and test and transfer knowledge.

# How to Coach the 5Ps

To have a successful innovative team coaching experience, there are some basic requirements, rules, and a process to conducting team meetings. Distilled and adapted from the work of Reg Revans, introduced in chapter 4, and Marquardt's follow-on research and teaching, here are the requirements that derive from the action learning process. (**Note:** See the appendix for a deeper analysis of the Innovation Development Process rules, with an easy-to-follow scenario and follow-up guidelines.)

- Gather a team of four to eight people who need not be experts in the problem area; however, having one or two participants who have a solid background in the area is highly suggested.
- Include a leader-coach with experience in leading action learning groups or at least some coaching experience who is willing to follow the process.
- Present a problem or opportunity that has no single solution but is important to the organization—a problem open to a creative solution that can be later forged into an innovation.
- Use an inquiry model with powerful questions that require reflection, listening, and respect; key are who, how, what, and open-ended questions.
- Follow the 5Ps Innovation Development Process: problem, present, possible, plan, and pivot.
- Show strong interest in solving the problem and taking action.

When we last visited Epps Security, the detectives had settled on their collective vision, sweetened by a no-interest credit loan from a very satisfied customer, and while, with the help of their coach, they'd asked themselves some existential questions, they had no idea how to pivot.

# THE STORY: The Agency Innovates, or Time to Pivot

"We've been hacked!" said Bill peering into an email on his smartphone. "That's the only explanation," he muttered as his fingers scrolled faster.

"What are you talking about?" Jenn looked up from her laptop from across the room. She was never sure about Bill. He didn't seem comfortable with the younger employees, maybe it was her, or was it everybody? He was just an old-fashioned PI, like the monotone cop sidekick on the late-night rerun TV police dramas like the original *Hawaii Five-0*. ("Book 'em, Danno." She was sure that Bill had said that once.) But IT was her baby, and if there was a problem, it was hers and hers alone.

"I've got emails from some guy I've never heard of about someone he shouldn't know. Do you know what I'm talking about?" Bill asked as he strode across the office toward her, phone in hand. "This somebody's got info about a confidential source. How could that happen?"

"It's not possible. All our important data's on the cloud."

"Are you talking money or people?"

Jenn paused. "Our customer data is where it should be, employee records, too." But she knew this was a different group, confidential sources, a group that wasn't. Was it possible?

"This whole operation lacks security. I knew it!" Bill fumed. "You've got these kids coming in here at all hours, I have no idea who they are! You can't set up a company with the security we built our careers on, pure and simple. Our confidential source could lose everything over this. We could be sued!"

Just then Roland walked in. "Who could be sued? What's up? What happened?"

Jenn took a deep breath and exhaled. "Bill got an email and thinks we got hacked."

Roland tipped his glasses down over his nose and peered at his partner. "Really? Like a Nigerian prince email?"

"You make me sound like a hick!" Bill bellowed. He was pacing now. "This is what I was afraid of. You take for granted what our badge gave us. Every time you walked through that department door, you entered a level of security that this little office can't match."

"Now hold on, hold on!" Roland raised his hand as much to stop his friend's movement as his harsh words. "Let's sit down and you tell me what happened." Roland walked over to the new beige leather sectional sofa, still pushed into the corner where it had been delivered six months ago, patted the seat and motioned to Bill. "Sit. Here."

"This is getting weird. Mind if I leave?" Jenn stood at a distance, arms on her hips.

"Yes, I mind! Come on, you too," Roland patted the seat next to him for Jenn. "Bill, you have the floor."

"Like I said." Bill spoke in whispered tones as if trying to contain further damage. "I got an email from an attorney in Florida wanting to confirm the whereabouts of an ex of one of her clients. I don't know how this person knows me or connected me to the ex, who has been one of our CIs for years."

"That's it?" Jenn stood up impatiently. "That's nothing. Would you even reply to such an email as a cop? Did you check out the attorney's credentials? Did you contact your source?"

"She might have a point, Bill," Roland said. "The other thing is, we're the new kids on the block, somebody could just be phishing. You know how that works."

"I don't need a kid telling me how to do my job." Now Bill stood up. "It's hard for me to keep track of all the caseloads. Accounts are kept here and there. Everybody's pulling files for whatever reason. I don't think you train people, Jenn, at least regarding sensitivity of client information. Stuff is all over the place."

"We've hired some contract investigators, you know that, and it's true that some of them work odd hours. But you've jumped from a specific email issue to a general problem with me, is that it?"

"I don't think he means that, Jenn," Roland interrupted, leaning forward.

"No, I do mean that," Bill said. "I said what I mean. And you," he pointed at Roland. "You're too freewheeling, too trusting, to run an agency like this. You need somebody like me to keep this stuff grounded, but now there's too much of it for anyone to look after. Stuff falling through the cracks that you don't see. I think Dana saw the possibility of these problems before we did. You just saw the fun."

"You're right," Roland said, "about the fun, I mean. But everybody here should have the fun, too." He smiled weakly at Bill, who shook his head.

Roland had to admit that much of what Bill said was true. Cases were coming in like sea water over the gunnels of a ship. They had to decide what they wanted the company to become. They could take everything that came in and add investigators, or they could set priorities. They needed Dana's help.

From the sound of Roland's voice on the phone, Dana assessed the group's urgency and offered to come by that week and establish a schedule of regular meetings.

At their first meeting later that week, the group gathered around Dana at the conference table. This was the first time they had met in weeks. Roland and Bill sat at either end, with Jenn, Dan, Rachel, and Ryan spread out among them.

"Coaching is all about asking questions," Dana said. "It depends on helping the person or group being coached to determine the problem, the present state, the possible future state, and plan going forward."

She then told the group about English researcher Reg Revans, who in the 1940s observed Nobel prizewinning scientists in their laboratory. They asked a lot of questions of each other, using an informal but rigorously applied process, which Revans called "action learning" because as the scientists talked among themselves, they learned how to listen. And, as people solve organizational problems, Dana said, they in turn learn a lot about leadership.

According to Dana, action learning answered difficult problems best, like what direction the group should take the company in the future.

"Revans thought that people don't make progress until they recognize that they have difficulties in what they're doing," Dana said. "In fact, to speak at the research lab you had to admit that your work wasn't going as well as expected."

"That must have been one cheery group," said Roland. His own group was silent around him, and he was uncomfortable.

She looked around the table. "So . . . think about that. What's not going like you expected?"

To a person, the investigators of Epps Security sat mute. Then Jenn spoke softly, "It's just that to build a business, to deal with a public, new customers, we need to be very upbeat; we have to believe we can get the job, every job, done. We can't even think about failing."

Roland looked across the table at Jenn, smiled, and thought, *Way to go, kid.*

"Don't see it as failure," Dana said, leaning across the table toward Jenn, and added softly, "Think difficulty. . . . We'll come back to this."

"Oh great," Roland moaned.

Next, along with coaching and action learning, Dana said that entrepreneurship research by folks such as Steve Blank, Erick Ries, and Clayton Christensen had produced a process that focused on customer development, and when entrepreneurship was fused with action learning, it produced a much more powerful process, the 5Ps Innovation Development Process: problem, present, possible, plan, and pivot. This, Dana promised, Roland's team would take up at their next weekly meeting.

And that next meeting came around fast. The entire staff—Roland, Bill, Jenn, Dan, Rachel, and Ryan—sat around the conference room table waiting for Dana, who was never late.

"So sorry!" said Dana as she breezed in. "Crazy traffic, but I come bearing gifts." And she emptied out on the conference table the contents of her red microfiber tote: *The Innovator's DNA, HBR's 10 Must Reads on Innovation, Innovation and Entrepreneurship, The Innovator's Dilemma, Start With Why, The Corner Office*, and *Smarter Faster Better*.

"Remember," she said, "'Not all readers are leaders, but all leaders are readers.'" As everyone looked up at her quizzically, she replied, "Harry Truman." Then she looked around the table. "Ready to innovate?"

First, Dana explained the rules:

1. No one could speak unless in response to a question. Thus, no impromptu advice or speeches. Anyone could ask a question.

2. As the coach, she could stop, start, or introduce a question to the group. She would not be a member of the problem-solving group—but would coach it to a solution.

Following the rules of the game, Dana reviewed the 5Ps Innovation Development Process with the team and explained that Roland, as the owner and founder, would serve as the problem presenter and get up to five minutes to articulate the problem.

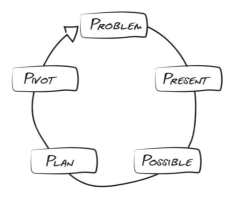

Roland started. "Look, we've become the victims of our own success. Business is coming at us from every angle—private, corporate, and the government." He went on to describe his frustration with the company's lack of focus. As the managing partner, he felt like the company was "all over the court."

"What did you really want the company to become?" asked Ryan. "Are there certain investigations you prefer? What's the real problem?"

"That's a lot of questions. Can he ask a lot of questions?" Roland looked to Dana imploringly.

"I think we'll say yes, for the time being, but it's best not to stack questions," replied Dana.

Whenever one of them started to give advice, Dana would cut in and politely say: "How might you ask that as a question?"

After about 15 minutes, Dana faced the group: "OK, you've been talking about the problem for a while. Please take a moment and every-body write down in a sentence or two what you think the real problem is."

Then Dana asked each of them to read exactly what they had written down. The rule was that they could not just speak freely; rather they had to read only what they had written. She explained that kept them from getting lazy and hitchhiking on each other's idea. That was for later. Now they needed to understand the problem.

Ryan read his first: "I think Roland is unsure of what he wants the company to become."

Jenn was next: "The current business model is unsustainable."

Bill: "It feels like we're drowning in our own success!"

Rachel reflected: "But isn't there a danger of being too focused, not being nimble enough to respond if conditions change?"

Roland turned to Rachel. "Like? Give me an example."

"External things," Rachel said. "Corporate clients downsize, the regulation landscape changes, some big firm from out of state invades our territory."

Dana then asked Roland who came closest to what he was thinking.

Roland hesitated and then said, "They all help my thinking. If I had to pick one that was closest, it's Rachel's. But if we pick a clear goal to work on, it would give us focus and direction. We wouldn't take on everything and would not feel like we're drowning."

Dana asked, "So can you sum up the problem for the team?

Roland said, "Incoming cases are overwhelming us; so, we need clear investigative priorities to work toward for the agency to thrive in the future."

Dana then announced, "OK, let's move to the second step—the present state. What questions does the team have regarding the present state of incoming work, what's going on right now?" Dana reminded each of them that they could ask each other questions as well. Questions need not be restricted to Roland.

In fact, Roland asked the first question: "Bill, you see most incoming cases, off the top of your head, what are you seeing mostly?"

"A lot of small—one-off cases—about 70 percent of what we're doing."

Roland explained to Dana that in general, these were smaller, chip-shot, less-than-a-few-days kind of investigation cases.

Ryan: "So, how does that affect things?"

After about 15 minutes of discussion, the group got quiet—as if they had finished this part of the process. So Dana asked, "Roland, can you summarize what you heard about the present state?"

He took a breath, looked up, as if searching for words, and said, "The present state," he paused and repeated to buy time, "the present state is . . . umm . . . well frankly to me it's overwhelming, frustrating, and not sustainable." Then Dana injected herself. "OK, let's move to the next P on the chart," she said pointing to the possible future segment on the whiteboard. "What are your ideas about the possible future of this problem—setting priorities for the company?"

The discussion started slowly. So Dana said, "Maybe this is a good time to break out of coaching—do some brainstorming just to prime the pump, would that help the group?"

Everyone nodded.

"OK, take a minute and write down some words—the first ones that come into your head." After a minute, she asked, "What did you come up with?"

Words popped out—profit, efficiency, training and development, corporate security, government contracting, counterterrorism, cybersecurity, identity theft, and fraud.

"OK, looks like we've got some good ideas out. Let's go back to coaching and questions. Who's got the first question?"

Jenn's hand shot up: "Ryan, tell me more about your thinking about corporate security."

Ryan went on to explain, that rather than take in private cases, they'd be much better off getting a long-term, retained contract that allowed them to develop a strong financial base.

Then Bill jumped in, "From a billing and admin perspective, it's the best route for us to go."

Dana interrupted, "How can you put that as a question?" Bill stammered and said he'd hold off for now.

Dana pushed him, "Can you ask that as a question that might engage others?"

Bill thought and then said, "OK, besides the relief in billing, are there any other efficiencies that might come from larger, retained clients?"

Dana laughed out loud, "Boy, you finessed that one—got your answer in and tossed to the group!"

After about a good 45-minute discussion on the possible future, the group had come up with three possible paths: forensics analytics, corporate security, and corporate espionage.

Then Dana injected, "OK, let's move to the planning segment. Who is willing to do what over the next two weeks to explore these three areas?"

Ryan and Rachel volunteered to explore corporate security. Jenn raised her hand to take corporate espionage. Dan shrugged, smiled, and agreed to take the only remaining topic, forensics—his specialty.

Bill volunteered to check and categorize the kinds, numbers, and revenue that had come in during the past year and to put together a spreadsheet. He then demurred. "You know, these are really big issues, with big expenses. What about the kinds of cases we cut our teeth on as cops? What about the missing persons, for example? Cops are understaffed for some of those kinds of long-running cases."

"You're thinking about that birth parent case a couple years ago, aren't you?" As Bill nodded, Roland explained to the others, "Bill and I took on this case privately, as a favor to a CI, and it had one of those outcomes that pleased everyone." Roland shook his head, smiling at the memory.

"I still hear from both Marcy and her daughter every year," Bill said.

"Look, I think we should continue to do those kinds of cases," Roland said, "but they're time consuming, as you well know, and I don't see how on top of that load you'll be able to do all the admin stuff you've been doing."

"I can help out there," Jenn piped in and raised her hand for emphasis. "Really, would be my pleasure."

"Actually, those kinds of cases could involve a lot of medical research—right up my alley," added Rachel.

"So," summed up Roland. "I'll call up a couple of our CEO clients and a few other trusted friends, ask their opinions on some next steps to help us grow."

Dana asked them to check their calendars and set a meeting for two weeks, which they thought would give them time to work.

"Hey, Dana, I have a question," said Dan, the vigilant accountant. She nodded, so he continued, "I'm looking up at what you posted at the start of the session—why aren't we discussing the pivot?"

Dana explained that pivoting would come at the follow-up meetings when people had gone out and tested various questions about forensics, corporate security, and espionage. "More knowledge may well redirect your thinking and the team's direction."

"You mean like finding out there's no Santa Claus?" Bill scoffed.

"Or better that there is a Santa Claus—your parents!" Dana joked.

Bill nodded and everyone laughed.

But before she let them go, she asked them to write down the answer to two questions: What did you learn? What was of value?

After going around and hearing encouraging words of progress, understanding, and engagement, Dana said, "Thanks, see you guys in two weeks."

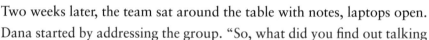

Two weeks later, the team sat around the table with notes, laptops open. Dana started by addressing the group. "So, what did you find out talking to others, especially clients?"

Jenn reported that she'd spoken to a couple former classmates who were corporate espionage analysts who used private firms to supplement their work, especially during their heavy seasons. She also talked to five of their largest clients—with some help from Bill and Roland—and had come up with a half dozen questions to conduct a quick survey and follow-up calls with them. The results were more than promising. Two of them said they'd entertain a proposal from the agency immediately.

"As for corporate security," said Rachel, "Ryan's and my initial assessment is that some property and facilities clients might involve too much capital outlay. For now." Ryan smiled. "We just need to narrow our focus," he added.

Next up was Dan, who reported about forensics. He had reached out to friends and colleagues both in IT and law enforcement who detailed a wide range of needs for data analysis in business processes—one of whom offered Dan a well-paying position doing exactly what he had just described. "Crazy," said Dan, shaking his head. "He thought I was looking for a job."

"Are you going to take it?" Jenn asked quickly before anyone else could muster a response. "I mean, you've only been here a couple months; we'd all understand."

"Says who?" Roland spoke up from his end of the table. Silence ensued. "Of course, Dan, you should do what you want, what's best for you."

Then Bill reported on client trends over the last year. He pulled out a spreadsheet. "OK, at a macro level, we're 80/20—small to large company. We take on many small, one-shot deals." Bill had documented what the team thought. However, he showed that the 20 percent of big companies represented 50 percent of their income.

"I knew it had to be significant, but I had no idea how significant," Roland said.

After some discussion, Dana put the group back into action. She posted the 5Ps again and said, "Let's start this time with the pivot step," pointing at the chart on the wall. "Looking back at the original problem that Roland confirmed, how have things changed? What's the problem look like?"

Everyone agreed that Roland's initial description that the current way of doing business was overwhelming, frustrating, and not sustainable.

Dana nodded, "Yes, and how has what you found in your exploration informed that?" They eventually all agreed that the present state had changed due to the new information—notably the data that everyone had brought to the discussion. And, maybe even more important was what Bill had discovered about the amount of revenue.

"So, would you say that the problem has changed—maybe even pivoted?" asked Dana. To which the group collectively groaned!

When the team came to the possible future segment, they brainstormed all sorts of options, from focusing on all three priorities—corporate security, industrial espionage, and forensics analysis—to focusing on just one.

This discussion had lasted about two hours when Dana asked what the plan was going forward—who might do what for the next meeting.

Roland asked Ryan, Jenn, and Dan to consider doing a back of the envelope plan for each line of their potential business. He also asked Bill to look them over and calibrate them on a level playing field. Just make sure there was an independent eye looking at all three. Bill strongly suggested continued contact with clients, strategic partners, and anyone whom they considered key stakeholders in the company's success to include on their own teams.

Once the meeting ended, Rachel and Jenn gathered up into Dana's tote the innovation books that she had lent them at the last meeting, looped the handles through their arms, and the three women walked out together, calling out good-byes as they left. Roland responded absentmindedly as he rolled down and smoothed his shirtsleeves, then watched through the large bay window as Dana, Jenn, and Rachel drove off together.

Bill and Ryan wordlessly scrolled through their smartphones. Dan straightened chairs, while near him Roland gathered coffee cups and jottings and notes left on the conference table.

Roland looked around the table, distracted. "Wasn't my wallet here?" Patting his jacket pockets, he asked Dan, "You hungry? Come on, I'm buying."

A couple weeks later the group gathered for another round. Using the same format, they began with the pivot—each reported the results of conversations with critical clients, peers, partners, and their own teams.

Essentially, Ryan found that there was plenty of corporate business that they were big enough to handle. By his projections and Bill's confirmation, the revenue stream could be significant.

Rachel added that, surprisingly, the competition seemed focused more on one-off cases and working with attorneys and the court. "It means we can be more balanced, pursue corporate customers while trying to get established among these older law firms."

Dan found a similar net result, and Bill vouched for the size of the pot available out there. However, he reported that the company would have to make a significant investment in personnel, equipment, and training to make a real dent in industrial espionage.

Dana then said, "OK, back to the process. Who has the opening question about the present state?"

Roland asked the group: "So after all this, what's our problem now? It's not *if* we should shift to a priority but *when*. Seems like now the question is which of these three would be the best place to dip our toe into a strategy."

Ryan, Rachel, Dan, and Jenn agreed with the definition of the problem as selecting a priority from the three topics addressed by the group. Then they discussed and reviewed the present state—what they'd covered in the past two meetings to create a level-set mentality before discussing the next step.

When discussing the possible future, the group passionately asked questions with Dana refereeing.

"Corporate security is so wide ranging," Rachel said. "From problems in the workplace like violence, to employee screening and privacy issues, business continuity planning, and cybersecurity. How do we staff for all the possibilities?"

"Good point," said Ryan. "I think we should consider getting some people with a legal background; others with management staffing expertise."

"I have an idea. May I offer a thought, Rachel?" Jenn asked.

"Sure," Rachel said.

"I think we need more tech-savvy people," Jenn replied. "Cyber and communications security are a growing corporate threat."

"So are we really leaving behind some of our oldest industry contacts?" Bill asked this of Roland only.

"You're thinking of Lou, I know," replied Roland, "and the other clients we made in warehousing and transportation."

"Seems like you might see cases like Lou's as small stuff," Ryan said.

"No," said Roland firmly. "I'm attracted to the idea of corporate clients, for sure, but we can never forget the Lous."

Finally toward the end of the two-hour session, Roland asked the team to vote privately for each of the three—based on the company's financial situation, which he and Bill had been transparent about. He also asked them to consider whether they could do only one, two, or all three. He also asked them to consider alignment of the company's current resources that could be leveraged. They voted on small pieces of paper that Bill handed out—giving three points for the first choice, two points for their middle choice, and one point for their least favorite choice.

Bill handled the scores and the math when they came in. The findings were clear: the number one choice was corporate security, number two by some margin was forensics, and last was corporate espionage.

Dan and Jenn were disappointed with the results but could not argue with the findings.

Roland asked, "OK, what should we do now?"

Ryan said, "Test our findings with our major clients, staff, and others—just to make sure we're reading things correctly."

The next meeting took place two weeks later. And a month after that the team rolled out a three- and five-year plan that included focus on corporate security with continual assessment of both forensics and corporate espionage, with an eye to moving toward either or both of them as company resources grew. There would always be room for smaller cases, everyone agreed, especially now that they had a few larger corporate retainers.

"Those cases are our legacy," Roland said to Bill, "as cops, as partners, who we are."

"Like I said before," said Dana, "Such romantics. But nice sentiment."

"All this reminds me," said Roland turning to Dana. "Did you ever get a call from Lou?"

"Ah," replied Dana feigning coolness. "Privileged client information, Mr. Epps." She then smiled. "Mr. Spagnolla speaks highly of you, too."

## Roland's Notes

- [ ] People on the team have very different views of what the real problem is.
- [ ] You can't change a system without changing yourself.
- [ ] Problem, present state, possible future, plan, and pivot.
- [ ] Pivot in the direction of customer needs.
- [ ] The individual learns by participating in the inquiry and action to solve the problem.
- [ ] The group learns as it faces the problem, answers questions, and adds to its knowledge base.
- [ ] The organization learns as group members spread the learning-and-inquiry process throughout.
- [ ] Leaders will have to push some more than others.
- [ ] What's the cost of doing nothing?
- [ ] Questions, not answers, work best to solve problems.

# EPILOGUE

## Five Years Later: The Agency Matures

Roland, Bill, and Dana were having dinner in Fairfax at Roland's favorite restaurant, Villa Mozart, a quaint Italian place where the food was as good as any place in D.C. Roland had eaten there so often, he had a favorite table in a little alcove off the main dining room; a private place where he and Bill had very personal conversations with clients on many occasions. On this night, Roland, Bill, and Dana were celebrating.

As the three ate their soup that Oscar, the waiter, had brought them with a flourish of fresh-ground pepper, Roland lifted up his wine glass and toasted, "Here's to the agency and all the hard work that we have done to make it happen."

"Special thanks to you, Dana, for being our guide," said Bill, as his glass touched hers.

Dana nodded in appreciation, cleared her throat, and spoke: "You guys have done a great job building an intentional culture of innovation." She congratulated them for developing a place where people felt safe and secure to try new things—to experiment. And how that environment had fostered great innovation and kept their agency in front of the pack. She also praised them for continuing to use the 5Ps Innovation Development Process. "You guys kept asking questions of each other—"

"That was Roland, especially after the case of the . . . " Bill stammered. "When we got sued."

"Boy, Rachel was quite the undercover PI, wasn't she?" said Roland, shaking his head in wonderment.

"You guys were lucky. You never thought of making a deal?" asked Dana.

"Never. We didn't have that kind of cash. We would have had to close shop. Remember, they were our client," said Roland.

"So they just blinked first?" asked Dana.

Bill nodded. "Basically."

Roland filled in the details of the case: "It began when Rachel goes undercover at our client's request to check out suspicions of internal company theft. Then she happens to discover they just fired an employee who'd been diagnosed with a disorder requiring expensive treatment."

"An exemplary guy by all accounts," said Bill. "So Rachel copies the incriminating company files, and sends them off to the fired guy, anonymously of course."

"She returns to the office the next day," says Roland, "and promptly quits. Says she made a mistake, that she put her personal ideals before the client—acted unethically."

"Which is true," said Dana. "Although what the client did wasn't legal."

"Legal schmegal," said Roland, reaching for the wine bottle as the waiter glided over to fill his empty glass. "What matters is that Rachel found her true client—the poor guy they tried to screw out of his medical coverage."

"In fact, she actually went to med school and is becoming a doctor," said Bill proudly.

"Like I've always said about you guys, such romantics. You like the happy endings," said Dana. Roland smiled as the waiter poured more wine for Dana and then for Bill.

"You might say . . . we live to innovate," said Roland.

"Explain to me how that's innovation," said Dana.

"We talked it out, just like you showed us," said Roland "Every step of the 5Ps we did on the whiteboard that morning Rachel left."

"First, we had trouble deciding what the problem was, remember?" said Bill turning to his partner.

"Right," said Roland. "Is the problem that Rachel, who'd become a part of our team, is leaving? Or is it that we think we could be sued by a client for something she did?"

"So we ended up really thinking about our direction, our mission, thanks to her," said Bill.

"Ah, I see," said Dana, nodding to Bill and taking a small sip of wine. Then she turned toward Roland. "Hey, on another topic, Roland, you never did tell me how that newspaper column of yours came about."

"My notes," replied Roland. "I've kept them for my cases for years, but when we started working with you they took on a whole new slant."

"Roland started putting some thoughts together for our whiteboard meetings," Bill said. "Then when Jenn created our website, she posted one of Roland's notes there, asking questions about security and safety, personal and business, and coupling it with questions about risk—that we all ask ourselves—how do you define acceptable risk?"

"I was upset with her for doing that," said Roland. "It felt like such a personal breach—is that too strong a word?"

"Well, I've never heard you use it before," said Dana, feigning amusement.

"You were upset at first, and she apologized," said Bill. "Kids today just think differently than we do about what's private and the Internet."

With that Dana and Roland both burst out laughing. "Listen to you! Mr. Privacy on the Internet talking," said Roland shaking his head.

"But the upshot was that people responded," said Bill. "It just snow-balled. The editor of the local paper's business section got interested and the rest is history, as they say."

"I like writing, surprised to admit that," said Roland. "The column is good for me, connects me with people, ideas."

"Good for business, too," said Bill, and Dana smiled.

The three laughed, drank, and ate well that night and then called Uber for a safe ride home.

Indeed, a lot had happened over the past five years. The company now employed 20 people and had a gross income of a few million—beyond whatever Roland or Bill would ever have guessed could happen. They'd been approached on several occasions by even larger firms, but the two of them were having too much fun to do that—just yet.

Every employee now received a small but meaningful equity stake in the business if they stayed two years, and the team leaders got even more respectable equity shares. There had been promotions as well.

Dan was chief operating officer, now that Bill had joined Roland as co-managing partner. Jenn was chief administrative officer, handling the budget, human resources, and training and development. And Ryan, who had first joined the firm as a contract investigator, headed all field operations.

But what pleased the partners the most was how, after all these years, they had managed to stay loyal to their first clients, work and solve the kinds of cases that first attracted them to police work, and still grow their firm. Roland and Bill had essentially, and intentionally, created a little PI storefront, R&B Investigations, within the larger Epps Security. Dana called it an "elegant boutique solution," causing both Bill and Roland to howl with laughter.

Several days after the celebratory dinner at Villa Mozart, Roland and Bill were sitting in their office together after a long, productive day.

Bill stretched in his chair and said to Roland, "Hey got a serious question for you."

"Shoot."

"When do you plan on retiring from all of this?"

"Never."

"Seriously?"

Roland leaned back, "I am serious. I don't have a hobby, don't play golf, and don't have a family to come home to at night. I think I'd go stir crazy! How about you?"

Bill thought a bit and then said, "Not sure. May want to travel with Sandra. But still trying to figure that out."

"Well, whatever you decide for yourself will be the right thing, partner," Roland said.

Just then the phone rang. Roland picked it up and grabbed his note-pad. Bill could tell it was serious. Roland had that look and started scribbling—a client with a big problem . . . for sure.

### Roland's Notes

☐ What's the present state?

☐ Who's involved?

☐ What's been done so far?

☐ Keep one foot planted where you are and pivot.

☐ Remember, you can't change a system without

changing yourself.

# APPENDIX: CASE STUDY

Now that you have read about the 5Ps Innovation Development Process as shown by Dana, the executive coach, with Roland, Bill, and their private investigative crew, here is another scenario to illustrate the process and provide a template of sorts as you experiment with the process and apply it to your team and your organization.

## 5Ps Innovation Development Process Rules

Like action learning, the 5Ps Innovation Development Process is a team coaching experience that has a few salient rules—again, derived and adapted from action learning:

- A statement, pronouncement, or any pontification can only be made if responding to a question. No grandstanding or pushing one's own agenda.
- The coach has authority over the ground rules, the process, and learning. The coach can stop and start the process but does not participate in the solution itself.
- The coach owns the process, and the team owns the content.
  Thus, the coach doesn't enter into the discussion as a participant.

At its heart, this process not only solves problems and provides new opportunities, but it also teaches people the most important skills of great leaders: respect, humility, listening, asking the right questions, and the will to take action.

# The 5Ps Innovation Development Process Scenario

The leader-coach will ask a person with a problem or business opportunity to present or explain what he thinks is the problem or issue. Generally, the presenter should take no more than about five minutes to lay out the problem or opportunity. Then, the team should be allowed to ask questions of the presenter (and themselves) to help the team, and even the presenter, better understand and refine the core problem.

The coach should ask that participants take turns at note taking, with a different note taker volunteering for each session.

## Problem

Harry, the problem presenter, explains that the company needs a better evaluation system for employees. He describes how the ratings have skewed toward the high end of the scale over the past five years—such that 85 percent of people are given an outstanding rating—causing complaints within various departments.

Next, discussion about the problem or opportunity takes place. After about 15 minutes, the coach will stop the proceedings to see if everyone, including the problem presenter, fully understands the problem. To ensure common understanding, the leader-coach asks each team member to write down a description of the problem. Then the leader invites each member to read the description to the problem owner. If you skip this step or simply do it orally, people get lazy and follow the herd and say things such as, "I agree with what Mary said. . . ." Independent, diverse thinking contributes far more at this stage.

Questions come at Harry about the ratings and the raters. How long has this been a problem and when did it surface? The discussion leads to one about a lack of calibration among raters. There's no accountability or discussion among managers about who should get a high rating and why. Suddenly the problem shifts from examining a new system to confronting the old one—mainly managers explaining and defending their ratings to each other.

It's now useful to see how close the team is to a common understanding of the real problem—a most critical point in the process. Einstein once said, "If I had an hour to solve a problem and my life depended on the solution, I would spend the first 55 minutes determining the proper question to ask, for once I know the proper question, I could solve the problem in less than five minutes." Often, highly driven and motivated people—all champing at the bit—just want to solve the problem, regardless of whether they completely understand it. The leader-coach needs to find out what the problem owner thinks about these statements and which one comes closest to the problem owner's thoughts. Most often this step takes time but needs to be done right.

After much discussion, Harry agrees that the real problem is not necessarily that the evaluation system is bad, but that over time, the raters skew the rating toward higher scores to be the "good guys." There's peer pressure to ease up on people, rather than peer pressure to give accurate ratings. Thus evolves the real big issue, now reframed: How can we ensure that managers give fair, honest evaluations across the company in a consistent way?

However, if in the mind of the problem owner the team has not hit the problem squarely, the leader-coach should put the team back to work and do another discovery round until the problem owner is convinced that the team has its focus on the real problem at hand. Often, even the problem owner isn't clear, and the team inquiry helps her to better understand the real problem. In essence, problem identification is both essential and iterative.

Note that the team's inquiry process (that is, how the team interrogates the problem) should use the very same questions as in individual coaching: what, who, how, and open-ended questions. Again, it's critical that these questions get asked, rather than "yes-no" questions or directive questions (for example, "Have you thought of trying the XYZ process?"). Directive questions narrow thinking too quickly and can often quickly solve the wrong problem.

Once the issue or problem is clear, the coach leads the group through the other four stages of the 5Ps Innovation Development Process. Teams should err on the side of spending more time clarifying the problem. And while the coach will keep the team on track, the coach does not engage in problem solving, only in guiding the team through the process. The coach helps facilitate the team through each step and does not move on until there is agreement that the team is ready to take the next step. The following sections show how this example moves further through the process.

## Present State

Questions focus on what's going on currently at the company regarding evaluation. For example, how are managers held accountable for consistency? Is consistency and calibration valued in the company? Who are the best raters in the company—fair but firm? What do the data from the past five years show regarding the three levels of rating: does not meet requirements, meets requirements, or exceeds requirements. Such questions are asked until the group has a good baseline.

## Possible Future State

Next the leader-coach directs the team's attention to the best possible future state. What might the best future state look like for how to hold managers accountable? Leader-coaches who allow a lot of free thinking here get the best results. Much like brainstorming, this is the place for divergent thinking—not decision making. A list of priority items agreed to by the team will help the next step—planning.

## Plan

Finally, the leader-coach needs to bring the session to a close. Sessions can last from 30 minutes to two or three hours—usually the outside edge of people's attention span.

At some point, the leader-coach might point to the priority list and say: "OK, we have a great start and a list of to-do's going forward. So who will do what, by when, and how will we know it got done?"

When the team-coaching session ends following the planning-step discussion, the coach asks team members what they learned about leadership in general. Participants will often comment on how they learned to really listen, to respect others' opinions, and to be more patient. All these and other lessons are terrific for leadership maturity. Another way of asking a similar question more indirectly is to ask: "What one or two things of value did you get from today's team meeting?"

## Pivot

The final and fifth state in the 5Ps Innovation Development Process actually starts between the first and second meeting. It includes all team member activity, experimentation, and discussions, especially with potential customers. Where the team arrives back from the second Innovation Development Process meeting is often different from where it started. Remember Steve Blank's observation, "No business plan survives first contact with customers."

# Follow-Up Meetings

In follow-up Innovation Development Process meetings, the coach starts with an opening round during which each person reports what he or she found after engaging in research, inquiry, and experimentation. After the reports are finished, it's a good idea to test the problem to make sure it's remained the same or if it's changed based on the research by the team and exposure to customers. This is the pivot step in action. Remember that innovation is an iterative process—not a one-and-done process.

Thus, the leader-coach might ask team members to restate the problem concisely as they now see it, having done some research and run it by the customer. At this point, the leader-coach will ask them to write down the newest version of the problem-opportunity and read it out loud. If there's a new finding or twist about the issue, it's worth spending time making sure the problem gets reclarified before the team dives back into solutions. The coach might also ask about the present status of the problem—how is it going? Has it gotten worse, better, or is it about the same? Note that the coach is essentially going back over the 5Ps Innovation Development Process. There's no "normal," and the coach works with the team wherever it finds itself.

Next, the leader-coach asks the team to address the possible future state again. Has that changed? What are the priorities, given the new findings that team members brought back to the table? Note that the coach can stop and start the group based on what he or she senses is needed to make the process work for the team. For example, when a group gets stuck, the coach might say, "OK, it feels like we're stalled on this point. Would you all like to take a break and brainstorm for 10 minutes?" Or, "How about taking out a piece of paper and writing down how you're feeling right now? Please be as honest as possible." Toward the end of the follow-up meeting, the leader-coach will:

1. Ask team members what they will do before the next meeting to help address the problem.
2. Ask team members to describe how the session was of value in solving the problem.
3. Ask team members what leadership learning insights they are gleaning from the process (for example, listening, asking questions, reflecting more, being less judgmental, becoming a better follower).
4. Set the dates and times for the follow-up meetings. All should have their calendars handy.

To be sure, teams can run into problems, such as members who don't show and people who don't contribute. There are ways to deal with such bothersome issues, but the best way will always be for the leader-coach to "raise the issue," whatever it is, and ask the group how they want to deal with it. For example, if Joe hasn't attended the meetings, then the coach might say: "I notice that Joe hasn't shown up to the past two meetings. Should we discuss this as a team?" Teams are very capable of solving problems, and coaches have to be willing to live with team solutions.

# ABOUT THE AUTHOR

 Steve Gladis, PhD, is a distinguished executive coach, author, and speaker, and one of the country's leadership experts. Founder and CEO of Steve Gladis Leadership Partners—a leadership development company—he is the author of 21 books on leadership and communication. His company works with businesses, associations, and U.S. government agencies, and he speaks regularly at conferences and corporate gatherings. Gladis is on the faculty at George Mason University in The Mason Institute for Leadership Excellence and is a former faculty member at the University of Virginia. He also served as an FBI special agent and was a decorated officer in the U.S. Marine Corps. His most recent books are *Smile. Breathe. Listen: The 3 Mindful Acts for Leaders* and *Positive Leadership: The Game Changer at Work*. He lives in Fairfax, Virginia.

# INDEX